GOD'S WORD AND WORK

The Message of the Old Testament Historical Books

THE MESSAGE OF THE OLD TESTAMENT HISTORICAL BOOKS

GOD'S
WORD & WORK

by

Kathryn Sullivan, R.S.C.J.

published by
THE LITURGICAL PRESS, COLLEGEVILLE, MINNESOTA

Nihil obstat: John Eidenschink, O.S.B., J.C.D., *Censor deputatus. Imprimatur*: † Peter W. Bartholome, D.D., Bishop of St. Cloud. July 11, 1958.

Printed by The North Central Publishing Company, St. Paul.

To The Right Reverend Monsignor
John E. Steinmueller, S.T.D., S.Scr.L.
Consultor of the Pontifical Biblical Commission

FOREWORD

THE *Triumph of the Lamb* or the *Mystic Lamb* is one of Van Eyck's great masterpieces. The central panel shows the altar on which stands the Lamb of God whose death gives life to men. Around the altar are those whom He has loved and whom He has loosed from their sins: pilgrims, warriors, men and women from every walk of life. Close to the altar is a group of earnest men whose worship is enriched by a knowledge of sacred Scripture: in their hands rest open Bibles, their eyes are reverently raised in homage to the Lamb, "He who is, who was and who is to come."

At the beginning of *Mediator Dei*, Pius XII reminds men that it is "Thanks to the shedding of the blood of the Immaculate Lamb" that each one is now able "to set about the personal task of achieving his own sanctification, so giving to God the glory due Him." This task, the Pope explains, is beautifully fulfilled in the liturgy, which is "the worship rendered by the Mystical Body of Christ in the entirety of its Head and members."

The importance of Sacred Scripture in the continuation in the Church of the priestly office of Jesus Christ is widely recognized today. The growing interest in biblical studies can in part be traced to the Holy Father's encyclical *Divino Afflante Spiritu*. He urges commentators of the inspired word "not to apply themselves exclusively to expounding those matters which belong to the historical, archaeological, philological and other auxiliary sciences," but guided by the "declarations of the teaching authority of the Church, as likewise the interpretations given by the Holy Fathers," they may stress the theology of the individual books in order to help all the faithful to holiness of life and through their study of "the Divine Word, they may taste how good and sweet is the Spirit of the Lord."

To help in some way to fulfill these desires of the Holy Father, this book has been prepared.

It is hoped that readers will keep in mind an application of the Holy Father's recommendation that the literary forms of Sacred Scripture be respected. These studies of the historical books of the Old Testament also have their own literary forms — they are intended to introduce readers to the Bible and to show some ways in which the sacred texts have been used in the liturgy. They make no claim to be comprehensive or exhaustive. If within the limitations of their own literary form they can unlock some of the treasures of the inspired Word and the liturgy of the Church, they will have achieved their purpose.

Kathryn Sullivan, R.S.C.J.

Manhattanville College of the Sacred Heart
Purchase, New York
Feast of the Assumption of Our Lady, 1958

INTRODUCTION

OUR Lord began His public ministry of teaching by reading a Scripture lesson to His fellow townsmen in the synagogue of Nazareth, and then explaining it, with the introductory words: "This Scripture which I have read in your hearing is today fulfilled" (Luke 4:21). That "today" was not a matter of twenty-four hours; because Christ is present to His Church until the end of time, it is a day that will see no setting but leads to life everlasting, a day that should witness an ever growing discovery of Christ, in whom not only all Scripture but the total redemptive plan of God finds its fulfilment.

Whatever future religious historians may have to say about our era, they will certainly record to its credit an eagerness to return to essentials. Previous conflicts of the Church with various heresies could almost seem minor by comparison to the mortal combat with secularism in which she has been engaged in modern times. And when a great storm threatens, the roots of the tree must be deep and sound; the foundations of the house must be firm.

With the sure instinct that derives from the Spirit of Christ, His vicars on earth have therefore been urging His people to be built solidly on the Cornerstone. A new and wonderfully quickening awareness that Christ in the Church means Christ in the liturgy, and Christ in the Scriptures, has been the result. The emphasis on the Mystical Body since the Council of the Vatican, on Scripture study and prayerful meditation since Pope Leo XIII, and on the liturgy since Pope Pius X

—these are not three separate currents in the life of the Church, but a fresh and mighty flowing of the identical Wellspring of Life.

As early as the Third Plenary Council of Baltimore (1886), our own American hierarchy had called for a return *ad fontes*. "We hope that no family can be found amongst us without a correct version of the holy Scriptures. . . . It is not always feasible in the morning, but at least every evening, at a fixed hour, let the entire family be assembled for night prayers, followed by a short reading of the holy Scriptures. . . ." Under their sponsorship, moreover, a *Manual of Prayers* for national use was compiled containing the Sunday and feastday Mass texts, Sunday Vespers and Compline, the translation of the sacramental rites, various blessings, and psalms, liturgical hymns and sequences for devotional use. We are but now beginning to catch up to their leadership.

When at the Milwaukee National Liturgical Week in 1954, I invited Mother Sullivan to write a series of articles on the books of the Old Testament for readers of WORSHIP, I asked her to do two things: to help the "amateur" Scripture student discover how the Old Testament writings bear witness to Christ (John 5:40); and to convince him how imperative such knowledge of Christ through the Old Testament is to a fuller understanding and living of the liturgy. If the liturgical texts fail to convey their undisputed riches, a chief reason is that many of us do not know our scriptural A B C's.

How successful she has been became evident from the outset. Readers, with or without benefit of seminary courses in Scripture, wrote to express their gratitude. It was from these letters, moreover, that we learned how numerous were small "biblical circles" or study clubs, in almost every part of the United States. For the most part, their members had been restricting themselves to the New Testament, mainly because they considered the Old Testament too formidable. As one of the correspondents phrased it: "We need guidance to find the path through the underbrush." In Mother Sullivan's articles they were delighted to discover such a pathfinder.

Other volumes, aimed to help read and profit from the Old Testament books, have appeared in the meanwhile. Of such books there cannot be an excess, given the existing need. But we believe that none of them equals the present in so well and clearly delineating through the story of the Old Testament the person and saving activity of Christ, both in history and in liturgical Mystery.

Godfrey Diekmann, O.S.B., Editor of WORSHIP

CONTENTS

GOD'S WORD AND WORK

The Message of the Old Testament Historical Books

THE BOOK OF GENESIS

GENESIS means a beginning. The first book of the Bible is well named because it tells the story of the beginning of the history of the world (chapters 1–11) and the beginning of the history of the chosen people (chapters 12–50): the beginning of the work of God in the world and in the souls of men.

These two histories have a single theme. God's love is the meaning of the creation of heaven and earth. His love, too, alone can explain the selection of a special people, the making of a covenant with them and the great promises given to them and fulfilled in our own day.

In prose that is direct and unadorned, the most ancient traditions of the Hebrew people are presented under the simple imagery of an oriental and fundamentally religious race. Primitive history is related under four headings: the accounts of the creation of man, his fall, the story of the deluge, and that of the tower of Babel. Patriarchal history is recorded in the biographies of Abraham, Isaac, Jacob and Joseph.

The literary forms in which all this is told are not those which we find in classical Greco-Roman or modern literature. The Biblical Commission states that the fundamental truths revealed by God are expressed in the simple, figurative language of primitive peoples. In this spirit these pages must be read.

A MOST ACCURATE RULE

Precious traditions have been enshrined in these pages. God is shown to be the great *Yahweh,* "He Who Is," a name that is ineffable and indi-

3

cates the divine essence; He is the *Elohim*, "the Strong One," a term telling man of a power that knows no cramping limitations.

Certain passages of this book stress the Hebrew love for ritual and sacrifice. Other passages reveal a theology of history centering about the covenant and the law which were given to man in love, and for which a service based on love can be the only answer. A prayerful reading of the book of Genesis, with a constant turning back to analogous passages in other books of the Bible, affords the best answer to the question asked by St. Benedict of those who are hastening on towards God: "For what page or what word is there in the divinely inspired books of the Old and New Testaments, that is not a most accurate rule for human life?"

This is the purpose of the book of Genesis, not to teach men the secret laws of nature, nor to provide men with history in the modern scientific sense of the word, complete with dates and bibliography, but as St. Benedict explains, "to give us a most accurate rule for human life."

It is this book that the Church turns to on Septuagesima Sunday when she begins the annual re-reading of the Word of God.

GOD'S CREATIVE LOVE

The Bible opens with the words: "In the beginning God created the heavens and the earth." At the summit of His creation stands man, fashioned out of the dust of the earth, as we are reminded each year on Ash Wednesday, yet made in the image and to the likeness of God and destined to live in friendship with Him. Tempted, the first man fell. Sin with all its consequences entered the world.

Man was condemned but he heard a mysterious promise. To the tempter God said: "I will put enmity between you and the woman, between your seed and her seed; He shall crush your head, and you shall lie in wait for His heel" (Gen. 3:15). This verse is the *proto-evangelium*, the original gospel, the first glad message of our salvation through Christ.

GOD'S MERCIFUL LOVE

In the light of the fulfillment, we see in these words a prediction of the ceaseless warfare of our Lady and her Son with the devil and those who do his work. Mary's divine Child one day was to crush and bruise the head of the serpent by overthrowing the kingdom of Satan. Dante, remembering the teaching of the book of Wisdom (10:2), placed Adam beside the Queen of Heaven in the golden glory of the mystic rose. Eve is at her feet. St. Bernard identifies our first parents for the pilgrim-poet in these lines:

> He who neighboreth [Mary] upon the left is that father because of whose audacious tasting the human race has tasted such bitterness. The wound which Mary closed and anointed, she, who is so beautiful kneeling at her feet, opened and thrust.

One of the most illuminating of commentaries on these first three tremendous chapters of Genesis is to be found in the *Creation*, an oratorio written with prayer and deep insight by Haydn. Studying the pages of the Bible and the words of *Paradise Lost*, the sixty-seven year old musician produced the great masterpiece of his life.

The overture is at first inarticulate in utterance and without perceptible melody. Order gradually replaces confusion and discords are resolved as the chorus in mounting enthusiasm bursts forth with the triumphant acclaim: "And there was light." Great choral hymns unfold the biblical story of creation: the beauty of the world, the dignity of Adam, the exquisite loveliness of Eve.

Then we reach the slow, majestic close in which we recognize the unmistakable notes of heart-breaking human tragedy. Yet above and beyond man's suffering, transforming and transcending all his pain is heard his song of praise. Solo voices are set like living jewels against rich choral and orchestral masses in the triumphant final hymn "Jehovah's praise forever shall endure."

GOD'S SELECTIVE LOVE

A selective process is plainly evident in the patterning of the book of Genesis. Of Adam's many children the fate only of the two eldest is described. Of Adam's descendants we are told the story only of the sons of Seth.

After the deluge only the one branch of Noe's family, the Semites, is followed. Abraham had many sons, some of whom became leaders of Arabian tribes, but their story is ignored and attention is focused on Isaac, the son of Sara. Isaac had two sons, Esau and Jacob. They were the fathers of two peoples, the Edomites and the Israelites. But it is the history of the latter alone that is of interest to the sacred writer. Jacob's twelve sons are shown to be the heads of the twelve tribes of Israel, and with Jacob's dying blessing for the future leaders of God's chosen people and the establishment of these people in Egypt, the book of Genesis comes to a close.

This book deserves to be read in its entirety. This reading will be profitable if we remember that in these pages we will find the simply told story of the great facts of the beginning of the world and the history of the people of God. These truths are expressed in the forthright language of the men and women of patriarchal days. To read their experiences with faith and sympathetic understanding is to reap, so St. Pius X says, a threefold fruit: spiritual delight, love of Christ and zeal for His cause. For this purpose these passages are recommended:

ABEL MACADAIM

In sixteen short verses the story of Cain's jealousy, his murderous intent, and the consequences of his act are starkly told. St. Ambrose warns us that Cain's offering, unlike that of his brother, was displeasing to God because he did not make his offering at once but "after many days," and he offered "fruits," not "first-fruits." Enraged because God preferred Abel's offering, Cain turned against his brother. Through his deed, death came into the world.

No further mention is made of Abel in the Old Testament. His place is in the New Testament and in the liturgy of the Church, for he was a good shepherd; he offered a sacrifice pleasing to God; he was the innocent victim of a brother's hatred; and as St. Augustine says, "with him begins the right glorious City of God." He is one of the first Old Testament saints to be venerated in the liturgy. In ancient Irish festologies he is hailed as *Abel MacAdaim*, "the son of Adam," or *Abel mormac Adaim*, "the great son of Adam."

In the litany said today beside the dying he is the first saint to be asked to protect the departing Christian soul. In the gospel read on the feast of St. Stephen we learn that our Lord praised Abel as "the just one," and a parallel is implied between Abel, "the first martyr" of the Old Law, and Stephen, the protomartyr of the New.

The analogy between the lamb offered by Abel and the Lamb of God offering Himself on the cross is clearly drawn by St. Paul (Heb. 12:24). In the preface of the consecration of an altar, God is asked to look upon the new table of sacrifice as He once was pleased with the altar which Abel, "the precursor of the life-giving mystery of the passion," sanctified with his blood. All the ancient liturgies make some reference to him in the eucharistic celebration. More modern is the allusion to Abel's sacrifice in the secret for the feast of the Most Precious Blood:

"O Lord of power, we pray through this divinely ordained mystery that we may draw near to Jesus, the Mediator of the New Testament, and renew upon Thy altars the sprinkling of that blood which pleads for us more eloquently than the blood of Abel."

THE DELUGE

Marriage between the religious Sethites, "the sons of God," and the irreligious Cainites, "the daughters of men," led to immorality. Noe, "the preacher of justice," vainly tried to warn men in God's name to forsake their sinful ways. They did not listen. He and his family alone were saved in the ark when the flood-waters covered the earth. St. Peter praises Noe for his holiness and proposes the ark as a type of the Church and the waters of the deluge as a type of baptism (1 Pet. 3:21).

Belief in a deluge is widespread, so it is not surprising to find that many cuneiform flood texts have been discovered. Eusebius copied a Greek version that he had found, and dozens of other accounts have since been identified by scholars working in the Near East. They show that the monotheism of Genesis has no counterpart in these uninspired accounts and that the Bible story predates the most famous of all these documents, the Gilgamesh Epic, by many centuries.

For more than a year Noe and his family lived in the great three-deck, four hundred and fifty foot houseboat. When the waters began to recede God ordered him to leave the ark with his family and all the animals. Then he built an altar and offered a sacrifice in thanksgiving for his deliverance. God was pleased with this offering and promised never again to send such a flood upon the earth. With Noe He concluded a covenant, one of a series of great alliances which renewed the bond uniting God and man. The rainbow is the symbol of this covenant.

LOOK UPON THE RAINBOW

The magnitude of the divine promise that the world would never again be destroyed by a deluge amazed St. Gertrude one Sexagesima Sunday, when she meditated on these words more than six hundred years ago.

The holy Benedictine nun felt impelled to cry out in wonder, asking eternal Wisdom how such a promise could have been made in favor of men who, God knew, were to fall into so many excesses and crimes.

The answer she was given, according to her devout biographer, is a luminous reminder of the graciousness of God's ways with men. The divine promise is meant to steady us in the calm of prosperity and to strengthen us in storms of adversity — we must always trust One who has so trusted us.

To confirm this first covenant that God made with men, He chose the rainbow, a universal sign, one that embraces heaven and earth and all that they contain. These concentric circles of the delicate colors of the spectrum are to be found in the visions of heaven granted to holy men of the Old Law and the New, a perpetual reminder, as Bossuet observes, of God's unfailing mercy.

Sirach tells us what thoughts ought to fill our hearts when we see in the sky the same sign that was given to Noe, Ezechiel and the Beloved Disciple: "Look upon the rainbow and bless Him who made it: it is very beautiful in its brightness. It encompasses the heaven with the circle of its glory, the hands of the Most High have displayed it" (43:12f.). It is the pledge of His love.

UNLESS THE LORD BUILD THE HOUSE

Men living after the deluge in the plain of Babylon made their homes of baked brick and bitumen. They planned a great city from whose center a tall temple-tower or ziggurat would rise to heaven. So vast a project could not be achieved without divine help, but in their effrontery they disregarded the truth expressed by the psalmist: "Unless the Lord build the house, they labor in vain that build it. Unless the Lord guard the city, they watch in vain that guard it" (Ps. 124:1f.).

God's punishment was swift; the tower was abandoned and "the conspirators" scattered. Vainly had they sought to introduce their own concept of human unity and to abandon the worship of the one true God.

Thomas Merton has written an allegory of this arrogant disregard of God and its divisive consequences. In a beautiful drama entitled "The Tower of Babel," he shows that the failure to complete the tower and the mass migration of the people that followed was due to a failure in communication, an inability to agree about a common project, an absence of true values.

This re-telling of the age-old story of disunity is a biting satire of man's efforts in a totalitarian state, but the drama ends on a note of hope. God's Word will one day be heard. Men who welcome His Word will find unity because His Word is holy and His Word brings peace.

ABRAHAM AND ISAAC

The name of Abraham, his absolute trust in God, his uncalculating generosity, his instant obedience, his trials and his rewards are recorded in both Testaments. No superlatives seem too great for the man who heard the words we would so much want to have addressed to us: "God is with you in everything you do."

When God spoke, Abraham left Ur with his family, his flocks, all his possessions. Obeying the divine command, he journeyed over to Egypt, then he moved back to Canaan where he was to prove worthy of the divine promises. God told him he was to become the father of a great people who would possess the land to which he had come and in his descendants all nations would be blessed.

Abraham waited. In God's own time a son was given to him. Then he was told to sacrifice the heir of all these promises. "The father of all believers" was equal to this challenge; with unfaltering trust he prepared to obey God's command. And it was done unto him according to his faith.

The Fathers of the Church have seen in Abraham's son Isaac a figure of the Son of God. Carrying the wood for the sacrifice, Isaac obeyed his father and was restored to life. Like Jesus, Isaac was "obedient even unto death," and so he was able to triumph over death. His marriage with Rebecca was blessed, and from their long-awaited son, Jacob or Israel, the people of God took their name.

JACOB AND JOSEPH

Our Lord shows Jacob to us seated beside Isaac and Abraham, honored with them in the kingdom of heaven. Yahweh Himself did not disdain to be invoked as "the God of Abraham, Isaac and Jacob."

Throughout the centuries Jacob has been more often blamed than praised. Men fail to recall that he is praised in sacred Scripture as "the just one," and wisdom is said to have guided him along right paths, showing him the kingdom of God and giving him a knowledge of holy things (Wis. 10:10). He is indeed a worthy father of the twelve men who were to be the heads of the twelve tribes of Israel.

Of all of Jacob's sons, Joseph stands alone. He, too, is a figure of the future Redeemer, for he was persecuted by his brothers, sold for

some pieces of silver, humbled in his suffering, lifted to a high position
and empowered to save his people. St. Bernard discovered in Joseph
of the Old Law a figure of Joseph of the New Law. The Abbot of
Clairvaux said:

> Remember the illustrious patriarch who was sold of yore
> into Egypt, and be assured that Mary's spouse has inherited not only his
> name, but also his chastity, his grace and his innocence. . . . The former
> was gifted with the power of understanding prophetic dreams; the latter
> was privileged to become the confidant of God's mysterious designs and a
> cooperator in their accomplishment. The one preserved grain, not for him-
> self, but for the people; the other was chosen to preserve, both for himself
> and for the world, 'the living Bread that came down from heaven.'

WITH EAGER AND JOYFUL COUNTENANCE

In a profound prayer recited by the priest after the consecration of the
Mass, the Church turns to the book of Genesis for examples of holy
men whose sacrifices were pleasing in God's sight, in order that we
may make our offering with some of the same purity of intention which
long ago filled the hearts of these biblical heroes.

Three figures are given us to be our models: Abel, who sacrificed
the firstlings of his flock and died because of a brother's hatred; Abraham, who spared not his only son in an act of heroic obedience; and
Melchisedech, who offered bread and wine to the most high God.

Christian iconography depicts these men and their gifts in the stiff
archaic figures of the gold and blue mosaics of the church of St. Vitalis
in Ravenna, a sixth-century work of art that marks the climax of the
best early Byzantine style. In the volutes is represented the antitype of
these men and their sacrifices: the Lamb of God, the first-born of many
brethren who was obedient unto death, and whose life-giving death is
daily renewed on our altars under the appearance of bread and wine.

Lest we be tempted to wonder why we, of the New Law, turn back
to the Old Law and recall imperfect and earthly sacrifices when on our
altars lies the infinitely pure and eternally pleasing Victim, let us reread
what St. Thomas said when a similar objection was raised in his day:

> Although this Sacrament is in itself preferable to all the sacrifices of the
> Old Testament, nevertheless the ancient sacrifices were very acceptable
> to God because of the devotion of those who offered them. Therefore
> the priest asks in this prayer, that this sacrifice be accepted by God because
> of the devotion of those who offer it, just as [the sacrifices of the Old Testa-
> ment] were accepted by Him (*Summa* III, 83, 4).

LIKE RACHEL, REBECCA AND SARA

At a nuptial Mass after the *Pater noster*, the bridal couple kneel before the altar for a further blessing. The priest begs God to make the bride like Rachel, dear to her husband; like Rebecca, prudent; like Sara, faithful and long-lived. She is admonished to pattern her life after the example of these holy women so that her marriage may be one of love and peace, purity and truth. These three models are wisely chosen. They can help the new bride.

"Life is only a small house," the poet has said, "but love is an open door." Through that doorway she can pass without fear, and journey trustingly along the path that opens before her, whether it lead her through the valleys or over the hills. For as Sara and Rebecca and Rachel discovered, God who blessed the beginning of the journey will see her safely to the end.

Sara, the wife of Abraham, loyally shared the great patriarch's trials. With him she left the comforts of Mesopotamian culture; with him she endured the hardships of a semi-nomad life; with him she prayed that God would send her a son. St. Peter found words of praise for her obedience. St. Paul asks us to imitate her faith.

Rebecca's prudence is charmingly portrayed in the scene beside the well where Abraham's servant seeking a wife for Isaac sees her for the first time. To his question: "If you please, let me drink a little water from your jar," she graciously replies: "Drink sir, and I will draw water also for your camels." Then with courteous reserve she bids him welcome to her father's house and at once discreetly withdraws to prepare for the guest who has made so long a journey.

Fine courage is evident in her willingness to leave her family and make her home in a strange land when the Lord indicated that this is His will for her. Modestly she meets her future husband; and it speaks well for her tenderness and tact that Scripture adds that, although Sara had just died, it was through the love that Isaac felt for his new bride that he was "consoled for the loss of his mother."

Beside a well Jacob, too, found a wife. *Rachel* was "well-favored and of a beautiful countenance," and he was to love her dearly until her dying day. Twice seven years did not seem too long a time to work in order to win his bride; the fourteen years of service exacted by her father seemed "but a few days, because of the greatness of his love."

Rachel's name is said by the Fathers of the Church to mean "vision of the principle" and they have always chosen her to represent contemplation because a contemplative soul is one who, in a kind of holy leisure or repose, is absorbed directly and immediately with divine love.

Her sons, Joseph and Benjamin, were especially dear to their father, who mourned his wife when she died, and raised a monument to her memory at Rama not far from Bethlehem. Her love for her children and their many descendants, who were to play so prominent a part in the history of Israel, led Jeremiah to choose her to personify all grieving mothers who refused to be comforted when their boy-babies were killed by Herod after the Magi had failed to report to him the whereabouts of the newborn King of the Jews.

Medieval congregations loved the tender-hearted Rachel, and they made her one of the leading characters in their Christmastide dramas when they re-enacted the story of the slaughter of the holy innocents. Rachel, accompanied by two consolers, slowly moved among the figures of the little choir boys "slain" on the altar steps of the church by Herod's soldiers. She refused to be comforted by the well-meant words of the sympathetic women, and she did not cease her lamentations until they had reminded her of the joys of God's kingdom which had been won by the little martyrs.

Had Rachel been allowed by the medieval playwrights to remain until the end of the drama she would have rejoiced when an angel appeared singing our Lord's gentle invitation: "Suffer the little children to come unto Me." Whereupon the holy innocents quickly came to life and in procession followed the angel out of the church singing gaily of their blessed fate.

IN THE DICTIONARY OF LOVE

Love enables us to transform obligation into oblation. It cannot change a bad act into a good one, but it can ennoble and transfigure all that is good in us, and in what we do.

Mindful of this, St. Ignatius asks the exercitant who has come to the end of the spiritual exercises to deepen the love in his heart by a series of deliberate affirmations. In a "contemplation to attain the love of God," the soul circles with an ever-narrowing radius about the mystery of God's boundless love which He has proved by a never-ending succession of gifts. At this sight, the soul is filled with gratitude, yet at the same time is compelled to acknowledge the limits of its own answering love.

These two themes — the greatness of God's gifts, and the ingratitude of man — recur constantly in the story of God's love for man that is unfolded in the book of Genesis. As in some great symphonic poem the first book of the Bible states, restates, develops and presents under many forms all the *leit motifs* that can be summed up in the lapidary phrase of the little catechism that a child can memorize and a saint can never fathom: God made me to know Him, to love Him and to serve Him in this world and to be happy with Him forever in the next.

Considering the examples of divine love as they are revealed to us in the opening chapters of sacred Scripture we are forced, as St. Ignatius foresaw, to want to make more adequate a return to God for all His benefits, to give what we owe Him not grudgingly, but to surrender to Him all that we have and all that we are with the total generosity of a love that is strong, selfless and unafraid.

Nor will past failures, present limitations or future difficulties daunt us because, as Robert Bellarmine, a great saint and son of St. Ignatius, wrote: "Love is a very wonderful and heavenly thing. In its dictionary you will hunt in vain for the word 'impossible.'"

THE BOOK OF EXODUS

EXODUS is the second book of the Bible. It tells the story of the going forth of the Israelites from the bondage of Egypt and the solemn proclamation of the covenant on Mount Sinai. It is to the Old Testament what the Gospels are to the New. It enshrines the central point of Old Testament history and it traces the itinerary of the Church through time, which is also the itinerary of the soul seeking God.

The Israelites left a land of servitude and sin. With God's help they passed through waters which gave them life and arrested the pursuit of their enemies.

Years of struggle followed. Longings for the pleasures they had renounced grew strong. God's gifts palled. Sense-bound, they were tempted to rebel against God's ways, as we, too, are tempted when our life of prayer seems to be like the wilderness, a land "bleak, pathless, and arid" (Ps. 62:2). But God is near during these times of purification as He was near our fathers in the desert. Of this we are reminded each day in the invitatory of Matins. We must not harden our hearts as they did, but we must follow the example of the wise author of the seventy-sixth psalm. Remembering God's goodness to the Israelites, he cries out: "O God, Your ways are holy: Who is as great as is our God?" And we can add: Of what then can we be afraid? Trust God and we will find that He will come to our help "in the opportune time" and He will guide us along paths of His choosing to the land He has promised.

This is the lesson of the book of Exodus. This is the lesson of fidelity

14

and abandonment which Moses learned during these years and which must be proposed to every beginner in the spiritual life and practiced until death by the saint.

Moses dominates the book of Exodus. In the Old Testament his name occurs more frequently than does the name of any other prophet. St. Peter, St. John and the Christians of the early Church venerated the great leader who prefigured Christ. A partial list of the monuments of the first centuries shows that in 199 different places the story of Moses' life was carved or painted for the edification of the faithful.

BELOVED OF GOD AND MAN

It is almost impossible to exaggerate the importance of Moses and Elias in sacred Scripture. The great lawgiver and the great wonder-worker were heroes whom every Jewish child early learned to love. So there is special meaning in the presence of these mighty men of God on Mount Thabor shortly before Christ's death. To strengthen three of His disciples for the painful ordeal that awaited them in Jerusalem, Jesus climbed the steep, twisting path edged with oak, mastic and turpentine trees, and there on the heights overlooking the plain of Esdraelon, transfigured with heavenly glory, He spoke to Moses and to Elias of His coming death.

Of Elias, the author of Ecclesiasticus has fine things to say: of Moses he can use only superlatives. "Moses," he tells us, "was beloved of God and men. . . . God made him like the saints in glory and magnified him in the fear of his enemies . . . He sanctified him in his faith and meekness and chose him out of all flesh."

So it is fitting that the Church propose him as our model during the days in which we, too, need to be strengthened for our journey up to Jerusalem. Of the six great men of the Old Testament whom the Church presents for our study during the season of penance, Moses is the last:

Septuagesima Sunday...............................Adam
Sexagesima Sunday ....Noe
Quinquagesima Sunday............................Abraham
Second Sunday of Lent................................Jacob
Third Sunday of Lent................................Joseph
Fourth Sunday of Lent...............................Moses

The passage from Exodus read in the first nocturn for this Sunday is filled with appropriate lenten thoughts. To Moses guarding his father-in-law's flocks near Horeb, the Lord appeared in the midst of a thorn bush aflame with fires which never consumed its low burning branches. To Moses, He revealed that His name is Yahweh, "He Who Is," Israel's strong protector, their warrior, their God. Moses was given the task of leading the people to freedom. What happened next may surprise us. Four times Moses refused. Four times the Lord insisted. This reluctance we might censure as a fault were it not for St. John of the Cross, who, with clearer vision, explains that Moses, like all souls advanced in spiritual ways, was diffident about accepting a position which would bring him honor while he would have welcomed one which would have promised him lowliness and shame.

At last he obeyed. He asked pharaoh's permission for the descendants of the twelve sons of Jacob to leave the delta lands where the Nile pours its silt-laden waters into the sea. For four centuries, ever since Joseph was governor of Egypt, this had been the Israelites' home. Now pharaoh feared and no longer favored this dangerous minority group. He would not allow them to leave even for a three day absence. Neither the eloquence of his brother Aaron who was his spokesman, nor the gift of miracles with which Moses was able to confound the court magicians, won the desired permission.

Signs of Yahweh's displeasure followed. From June until the following April, plague succeeded plague. Pharaoh would not yield. These nine plagues were phenomena natural to Egypt: foul water, frogs, mosquitoes, gnats, cattle murrain, boils, hail, locusts and finally darkness. What was not natural to any land was the way these disasters came at Moses' word and ceased at his bidding.

BLESSED INDEED IS THE NIGHT

Most appropriately each year at Christmas and Easter, the Church recalls the night of the Israelites' going forth. On the day before the liturgical celebration of the birth of our Savior, the introit for the Mass is taken from the book of Exodus (cf. 16:6f.), the mode is the lyric sixth, the treatment is simple and prayerful, the words are rich with overtones that only those who know their Bible can fully understand: "Today you shall know that the Lord will come and rescue us: tomorrow you shall see His glory."

In the hymn of the Easter Vigil, after the new fire has been blessed, the paschal candle lighted and the church is ablaze with light, the people rise, and the deacon sings the Easter hymn of praise:

This is the night in which our forefathers, Israel's sons,
Were led forth from out of Egypt's yoke,
Dry-foot through the Red Sea to their liberty. . . .
O blessed night, when Egypt was despoiled and Israel enriched!
O night when heaven is joined to earth and God to man!

This was the occasion of the first celebration of the Pasch which was intended to be an annual reminder to Israel that they had been redeemed by the Lord. Moses ordained that "When your children ask you, 'What does this rite of yours mean?' you shall reply, 'This is the Passover sacrifice of the Lord, who passed over the houses of the Israelites in Egypt; when He struck down the Egyptians, He spared our houses'" (Ex. 12:27).

These words conjure up memories of the night when the Hebrews, loins girt and staff in hand, stood in family groups about the table and ate the first paschal lamb with unleavened bread and bitter herbs. Then they set out, enriched with the wealth of the Egyptians which had till then been unjustly withheld from them and which was their due for the land and property they were leaving behind them. Following God, they entered a new life marked by special proofs of His protecting and provident love.

Today, to the pious Jew, the feast is still a reverently observed memorial rite. To the Christian for twenty centuries it has been all this and much more. Because of Christ's passage through death to life and the daily renewal on our altars of the sacrifice of the slain Lamb of God, the Old Testament feast is a type of which the Christian Pasch is the fulfillment. St. Paul in the epistle read at Mass on Easter Sunday tells us how we are to observe this annual feast: "Christ, our Pasch, is sacrificed. Therefore let us keep festival, not with the old leaven, nor with the leaven of malice and wickedness, but with the unleavened bread of sincerity and truth" (1 Cor. 5:8).

LINKS WITH THE LITURGY

The Israelites journeyed in haste. True, the pharaoh had ordered them to leave but they, knowing from experience that his was a vacillating nature, did not delay. They carried with them dough not yet leavened. This was the origin of their feast of unleavened bread. They remembered with gratitude that their first-born sons had been spared. This was the origin of the ceremony of the presentation of the eldest boy to God. It was this prescription of the Law, which was in no way binding upon them, that Mary and Joseph observed so faithfully when they carried their Son to the temple and offered Him to the Lord. Then they redeemed Him, that is, they bought Him back with five silver shekels. This incident is commemorated each year on February 2. An attentive reader of the book of Exodus will find many links like this with the liturgy.

Let us consider some of these links. During the veneration of the

cross on Good Friday are sung "The Reproaches." These are a dialogue
of Syrian origin between God and those who crucified Him. "For thy
sake I scourged Egypt . . . I led thee out of Egypt . . . I opened
the Sea . . . I went before thee in a pillar . . . and thou didst scourge
Me . . . and deliver Me to the chief priests . . . and open My side
. . . and didst hang Me upon the cross."

A second use of the book of Exodus is to be found in the Easter
liturgy. Beginning with the Vigil and in each Mass until the following
Friday the proper contains a direct quotation or an allusion to the story
of the liberation of the Israelites.

A third reference is to be found in one of the most beautiful of all
the collects in the missal, "For Those at Sea": "O God, who brought
our fathers through the Red Sea and carried them past mighty waters,
while they sang the praises of Your name, we humbly beseech You
increasingly to protect Your servants on board ship, avert whatever
might harm them and bring them by a smooth passage to the harbor
they are seeking."

THE BURNING BUSH

Souls in prayer long have pondered on the meaning of the bush that
Moses saw aflame but which was never consumed. From its blazing
branches (we would probably call the little bush a prickly hawthorn)
we can learn many lessons. Father Damasus Winzen, O.S.B., lists some
of these lessons in his valuable study of *The Symbols of Christ*. Ever
since Adam's sin the earth has yielded thorns which sacred Scripture
likens to sinners; the learned Benedictine suggests that we draw the
conclusion that God, who has been called "a devouring fire," shows
in this figure that He comes to disloyal and stubborn men, but not in
order to destroy them.

Jewish legends point out that the thornbush is the smallest of all trees,
yet God made use of it in His dealings with men, choosing it in preference to some fine, tall cedar. The meaning of the third sorrowful mystery deepens when we remember that men in return used thorns for the
crown they gave their Savior. Shame at this ingratitude must color our
recitation of the Great Antiphon of Advent: "O Adonai, . . . who
appeared in a burning bush to Moses . . . come and redeem us."

The perfect fulfillment of the figure of the burning bush is expressed
for us by the Church in the Christmastide antiphon which acclaims our
Lady's virginity before, during and after the birth of her divine Son:
"In the bush which Moses saw as burning yet unconsumed, we recog-

nize the preservation of your glorious virginity. Intercede for us, O Mother of God."

And the practical application that we can make is the remembrance that the divine love which is the fire that Christ came to cast upon the earth does not disdain to enkindle the least and lowliest of His creatures. Such a thought can renew our hope and make us very reverent in our dealings with one another.

WE WILL BE OBEDIENT

Centuries before this God had made a covenant with Noe. This was the first of the three great covenants. Noe was saved from a sinful people to be the head of a new people pleasing to God. The second covenant was made with Abraham. Abraham was taken from the pagan civilization of Mesopotamia to be the father of a people as numerous as the stars in the heavens, as the sands of the sea, as the dust of the earth. And from this people was to come the Messiah. The third covenant was made with Moses and the people of Israel. They were rescued from the slavery of Egypt, they were fashioned into a nation in the desert, they were led to the land God had promised them. The people of Israel freely accepted the covenant God offered. Thunder shattered the silence of Mount Sinai again and again. Lightning pierced the darkness, leaving the darkness darker than before. Moses entered the cloud-capped mountain to receive the Old Law.

In the morning Moses read its terms to the people and they said: "All the things that the Lord has spoken we will do. We will be obedient." This is the central point of the Old Testament.

THE BLOOD OF THE COVENANT

On hearing these words Moses took the blood of the sacrifice and sprinkled part upon the altar and part upon the people saying: "This is the blood of the covenant which the Lord has made with you concerning all these words." By this act God and the people were united by an alliance sealed with the blood of animals. This alliance was not meant to last forever. It was a preparation for a new and eternal covenant which God would one day make with all mankind. This new covenant would be sealed with the blood of His beloved Son, as we read each day in the words of the consecration of the Mass.

Almost immediately the Israelites were unfaithful. This was the first of a long series of defections. Tiring of Moses' long absence, they gave gold to Aaron and adored the calf which was fashioned in the image of

Yahweh. Moses interceded and God forgave them, as He will forgive all men until the end of time.

FASTING STRENGTHENS THE STRONG

In the second nocturn of the fourth Sunday of Lent, St. Basil does not allow us to make any mistake about the lesson we are to learn from this incident: "Fasting strengthens the strong . . . makes rulers wise . . . protects souls . . . brings courage . . . teaches gentleness . . . wards off temptation." Like a good teacher St. Basil gives an unforgettable picture of the austere, God-fearing Moses fasting alone on the mountain and the giddy, wine-soaked multitudes making merry in the valley below.

The same lesson is spelled out by St. Paul in the epistle (1 Cor. 10: 1–5) read in the Mass on Septuagesima Sunday: "Our fathers were all under the cloud and all passed through the sea . . . and did all eat the same spiritual food and drink the same spiritual drink. . . . But with most of them God was not well pleased." Our holiness is measured not by the graces God gives us but by the use we make of all that we have received. Months later, on the ninth Sunday after Pentecost, the Church reads the next verses from the same epistle (6–13). There we are told very plainly that we must study the Israelites' failure to cooperate with the graces of the Exodus, and amend our ways, because all these things "were written for our correction." The gift of the manna is a case in point.

TO ONE MORE, TO ANOTHER LESS

Across a great space of lagoon the Venetians can admire the white marble Renaissance church of San Giorgio Maggiore. Within its spacious walls are many masterpieces. In fact, the first impression the stranger has is that he has entered some cavernous, high-walled museum rather than a place of worship. One of the most remarkable of these art treasures is a vast landscape by Tintoretto which hangs near the high altar. Its subject is "The Gathering of the Manna." The dominant color of this well-integrated canvas is blue, the deep, clear blue of the Italian heavens on a sunny day. Ruskin observes that the skillful use of white sets off all the brilliant colors, so that they glow in this rich setting with a bright, jewel-like intensity.

Few artists have ever succeeded so well in preserving unity of composition while presenting so many separate groups of figures. Some of the Israelites are washing their clothes, others are sewing, or cobbling, or working at a forge. In a bored, mechanical way others are gathering manna.

A painter less powerful than Titian's contemporary would have shown us these men and women of the Exodus hurrying to gather the miraculous food, marveling at the divine bounty, looking incredulously into the blue sky as if to discover the source of the welcome gift. The record of their indifference contains a far greater lesson. Long familiarity can deaden our appreciation of all things, even of the divine. For forty years their food had been supplied with unfailing regularity. Long ago they had ceased to wonder or cry out: *"Manhu?"* which means "What is this?"

They had forgotten that these soft, white wafers having "the sweetness of every taste" were given to them only after the flour they had carried out of Egypt had failed. A salutary reminder that it is when we have ceased to seek satisfaction in temporal things that we are ready for divine. We know that the Israelites failed to find all strength and sweetness in this food because they could not bring themselves to desire it, and it alone.

Another lesson is hidden in a matter-of-fact verse that tells the measure of each one's gathering. "They gathered one more, another less: neither had he more that had gathered more, nor did he find less that had provided less." Is not the same true of the graces to be derived from holy Communion? To a Curé d'Ars, a Mother Cabrini, a Maria Goretti came the same food that may be ours. God's giving is never niggardly. It is limited only by our capacity to receive. Nor will this Bread vanish with the rising sun as did the manna. In the Eucharist is He whose delight it is to be with the children of men. No excusing answer have we to the question sung so poignantly on Good Friday during the veneration of the cross. "Because I fed you with manna in the desert, you smote Me with blows. O My people, what have I done to you? Wherein have I grieved you?" To be grateful for His gift is one form of reparation.

THE WHOLE CHRISTIAN MYSTERY

The book of Exodus contains, in a way, the whole Christian mystery: the creation of the people of God, their liberation, their training, their purification. In its teaching no other book of the Old Testament has greater richness or more dramatic variety, as the following passages prove:

GO FORTH, O CHRISTIAN SOUL

Exodus means a going forth. It is more than the title of the second book of the Bible, more than the name of God's great intervention on behalf of those He loved. It is a lesson every soul must learn. It is a program of sanctity. Abraham was told to leave his country, his family, the home of his father. The Israelites were told to exchange their settled life in a land highly civilized for a wandering life in the desert. They were freed from a pagan captivity and introduced to a whole new series of relations with God.

Long ago the old ritual of baptism made clear the prophetic meaning of the Passover. On the first Sunday of Lent the candidates were signed on the forehead with the sign of the cross, just as the houses of the Israelites were marked with the blood of the paschal lamb. The future Christians were told that through the saving power of Christ's blood they would be spared the punishment their sins had merited for them. Like the forty years the Israelites spent in the desert, so the forty days of Lent were to be for each candidate a time of trial. The Fathers of the Church expressed this plainly in their instructions. Let us quote Origen:

Know that the Egyptians will pursue you. They wish to bring you back to serve them. By the Egyptians I mean the rulers of this world and the evil spirits who once held you in their thrall. They will follow you in pursuit, but descend into the water and you will be saved. Cleansed from sin's soiling stains, you will rise, a new man, ready to sing the new canticle.

What is this new canticle? It is a canticle of victory. It is for those who are undefeated only because they have gone on trying. It is for those who know in whom they have believed. It is the canticle that the Israelites sang on the shores of the Red Sea when they escaped from the Egyptians. It is the same canticle that all souls will sing some day, when they have obeyed the last command that the Church will ever give them, a command for the final exodus: "Go forth, O Christian soul, in the name of God the Father who created you, in the name of God the Son who suffered for you, in the name of God the Holy Spirit who was poured out upon you."

That act of obedience will be our last victory over our last enemy, death. And as St. John has described it in the Apocalypse, in heaven standing on the shores of the sea of purest crystal, we will then sing "the song of Moses, the servant of God, and the song of the Lamb, saying 'Great and marvelous are Your works, O Lord God Almighty, just and true are Your ways, O King of the Ages. Who will not fear you, O Lord, and magnify Your name? For You only are holy. All nations will worship you'" (15:2–4).

THE BOOK OF LEVITICUS

LEVITICUS is the *Ritual* of the Old Testament. It contains the laws governing the sacrificial cult entrusted by God to the descendants of Levi and the rules regulating the daily conduct of the Hebrews whom God had chosen to be "a priestly kingdom and a holy people" (Ex. 19:6). It is the third of the five books which the Greeks called the Pentateuch, and the Jews, the Torah or the Law; these form the nucleus, as it were, of the Bible, for in them is found the story of God's love for man from the creation of the world until the death of Moses, the great law-giver.

MY SERVANT MOSES

Jews and Christians have long attributed the authorship of these five books to Moses. Evidence for this belief comes from Old and New Testament and is clearly evident in prayers still recited by Jews today. When Josue was told to lead Israel into the land promised to their fathers, the Lord added:

Play the man thou must, and keep thy courage high, carrying out faithfully the law my servant Moses enjoined on thee; never swerve to right or left, and thou shalt order thy life truly. The law thou hast in writing must govern every utterance of thine; night and day thou must ponder over it, so as to carry out all the terms of it faithfully; so wilt thou guide thy steps truly and prosper (Jos. 1:8f.).

Centuries later, when it came time for David to die, his last words to his son Solomon echo the same thoughts:

I am going the way all mortal things go at last; do thou keep thy courage high and play the man. Hold

24

ever true to the Lord thy God, following the paths he has shown us, observing his ceremonies, and all those commands and awards and decrees that are contained in the law of Moses; so shalt thou be well advised in all thou doest, at every turn of the way.

There are similar references to the law of Moses in the New Testament. Seventy-eight times he is mentioned by name and usually it is in some such terms as these: "Moses in the law . . . did write," or "As it is written in the law of Moses," and Jesus Himself appealed to the testimony of the first law-giver: "If you believed Moses, you would believe in Me; it was of Me he wrote" (John 5:46).

Mosaic authorship is still attested by devout Jews. Each Sabbath after the Torah has been read, as the scroll is held above the people, they recite a beautiful prayer in its praise: "This is the Torah which Moses set before the children of Israel. . . . It is a tree of life . . . those who uphold it are happy. Its ways are all pleasantness. Its paths are peace."

ADDITIONS TO THE LAW

While Jews and Christians continue to honor Moses, they have long recognized that his Torah has not come to them unchanged by the centuries. Cornelius a Lapide affirmed more than three hundred years ago that, "Moses wrote the Pentateuch simply as a kind of diary or record, but Josue or someone like him put these records of Moses into order, divided them into sections, and added and inserted some sentences."

The nature and extent of these inspired additions and insertions are questions of engrossing interest to the biblical world today. In a recent introduction to the Old Testament by a respected European scholar, seven hundred out of his nine hundred pages are devoted to this question of the composition of the sacred books and despite new documentary evidence, recent excavations and tremendous advances in all ancillary sciences, no definitive answer can yet be given.

Some historical additions are easily detected, for example the account of Moses' death that is found in the final chapter of Deuteronomy. More elusive are the legislative additions in Leviticus; but the legal codes of the Hebrews, like those of every nation, while preserving basic unity, must necessarily embody later enactments introduced to meet the people's changing needs. They are sometimes similar to the laws of neighbors facing problems so closely resembling their own.

A careful reading of Leviticus reveals a further complication. The book is seen to be no systematic exposition of statutes governing the ritual, social and personal life of the Israelites, but rather the combination of several incomplete collections of laws whose basic elements are Mosaic.

The background for the book of Leviticus can be quickly given. Out of Egypt God had called His people. They had entered the steppeland that was to be their home for forty years. At God's command they had erected the tabernacle with ark and altars and sacred vessels. When all was ready, a cloud covered the tabernacle and it was filled with the brightness of the divine presence.

Then it was that the Lord spoke to Moses, as we read in the opening words of Leviticus: "The Lord summoned Moses, and, from the tabernacle that bore record of Him made known His will. These rules the Israelites were to follow . . ." (1:1).

As we examine the twenty-seven chapters of Leviticus we see that these rules are of many kinds. Despite their dull, legal form they are well worth attention for they help us to understand much that is in the other books of the Bible.

First in position and importance is a collection of laws regulating the four chief sacrifices: the burnt-sacrifice or holocaust offered morning and evening and on great feasts, in which the whole victim was consumed by fire; the peace-offering or communion sacrifice, of which the offerer could partake; the sin-offering or trespass offering, which re-established friendly relations with the Lord when one had involuntarily or voluntarily displeased Him; and finally the cereal-offering, in which a gift of flour, oil and incense was cast on the fire so that its fragrance would be acceptable in the sight of the Most High (1–7).

The ceremonial of the consecration of Aaron and his sons then follows with an account of their solemn induction and a lesson on priestly sanctity (8–10). Laws of cleanness and uncleanness are enumerated with great detail and a purification ritual is prescribed with suitable modifications for various kinds of uncleanness (11–15). A festology follows containing the ceremonial for the Day of Atonement, the "Great Day" on which the Israelites begged God to look favorably upon them as a people despite any unexpiated private sins (16).

The next ten chapters are called the holiness code. This is less ritualistic in tone and provides for the conduct of priest and layman. There are additional regulations about sacrifices, certain prohibitions about marriage, definitions of religious and moral duties, recommendations about the domestic life of priests and people. There is also a liturgical calendar, rules about tabernacle lamps, laws for the sabbatical year and the year of Jubilee. The last chapter solves cases of conscience about vows and tithes. The book closes with this colophon: "Such are the commands the Lord gave Moses on Mount Sinai, to be proclaimed to the sons of Israel" (24:34).

LESSONS ALWAYS VALID

Leviticus is rarely read. And this is understandable. Much of its ritual is meaningless to the modern reader. Quaint and often crude are its dietary laws and the laws governing personal relations. Repetitions and stereotyped phrases do not attract even well-informed and well-intentioned readers who find much to repel or puzzle them. In his treatise on law, St. Thomas devotes questions 101, 102 and 103 to the Old Law's ceremonial precepts, their cause and their duration. Many of the objections his contemporaries asked him to refute are repeated today. Also to be repeated is the Saint's defense of all the many regulations Leviticus enjoins. He says:

The Jewish people were specially chosen for the worship of God, and among them the priests themselves were specially set apart for that purpose . . . so in that peoples', and specially the priests' mode of life, there needed to be certain special things befitting the divine worship, whether spiritual or corporal.

Now the worship prescribed by the Law foreshadowed the mystery of Christ. . . . Consequently, the reasons for these observances may be taken in two ways, first according to their fittingness to the worship of God; secondly, according as they foreshadow something touching the Christian mode of life.

In that spirit certain sections of Leviticus make rewarding reading. Father Frederick Moriarty, S.J., in his valuable little book *Foreword to the Old Testament* recommends the study of the Holiness Code (17–26), which he praises as "a well-rounded body of law regulating both liturgy and general moral conduct." In the *Bible de Jerusalem* it is suggested that Leviticus can be read with greater fruit in connection with the last chapters of Ezechiel or after the books of Esdras and Nehemias which give a true picture of life in a theocratic society. The author wisely adds: "Christ's unique sacrifice has made valueless the ceremonial of the old Temple, but the demands (of Leviticus) for purity and holiness in God's service are lessons always valid."

Perhaps the underlying purpose of the Law can be seen in still another way. To turn from the prescriptions of Leviticus to their application in other parts of the Bible is to understand something of the unity of the Sacred Books and the theocracy of Israel. Here are a dozen examples. An attentive reader will find many more.

To offer gifts	Lev. 4:3	Heb. 5:1–5
Aaron, Nadab, Abin	Lev. 8:1–10:7	Ex. 24:1–18
The first-born	Lev. 12:8	Luke 2:21–39
The leper cleansed	Lev. 14:2	Mark 1:40–45
Our High Priest	Lev. 16:1–34	Heb. 9:1–28
For the poor	Lev. 19:9f.	Ruth 2:1–23
Who is my neighbor?	Lev. 19:18	Luke 10:25–37
No other commandment	Lev. 19:18, 33	Mark 12:28–34
Honor for parents	Lev. 20:9	Matt. 15:3–6
God's people	Lev. 22:31f.	Ex. 19:1–25
Eye for eye	Lev. 24:17–22	Matt. 5:38
The law I love	Lev. 26:1–45	Pss. 18, 118

ALL MY PROMISES I WILL MAKE GOOD

A careful check of the Church's liturgical books shows that relatively little use has been made of texts taken from this liturgical book of the Old Testament. No reading is taken from it for Matins except the passage on the feast of Purification that contains the law our Lady so graciously obeyed when she carried "Jesus to Jerusalem to present him to the Lord." Some verses are chosen for the responsory of Passion Sunday, and on Wednesday in Passion Week the Church first prays that our hearts be enlightened, then reads the list of commandments that we must observe in dealing with our neighbor (19:1f., 11–19).

On Ember Saturday after Pentecost, in the ancient vigil ceremonies, two lessons are taken from Leviticus (23:9–11, 15–17, 21 and 26:3–12). Their words must have special meaning to those who are ordained during this Mass: "If you keep my law . . . all my promises to you I will make good." On Ember Saturday in September, two lessons are also taken from Leviticus (23:26–32 and 23:39–43). These are precise instructions about the observance of the Sabbath and other feasts.

Obviously the liturgical value of Leviticus to us cannot be limited to these few verses or to isolated ritual actions. Rather it is to be found in the great principles of expiation and substitution inculcated in the Old Law and realized in the fulness of their power in the New. Only to an all-holy God can sacrifice rightly be offered. Only by those specially set apart can this sacrifice be made. Only a perfect victim can be sacrificed. And since "Jesus is at once God giving Himself to man and Man giving Himself to God, being thus the confluence of the two loves," it

is "through Him and with Him and in Him" that we can give God
"all honor and glory."

SYMBOLS OF THINGS HEAVENLY

Usually those who love holy Scripture lament that so few share this
love. St. Jerome writing in 394 A.D. to his friend Paulinus has another
grievance. He finds that many men set about explaining the Bible, without due preparation and proper respect. He deplores the fact that, "the
art of interpreting the Scriptures is the only one of which all men everywhere claim to be masters." Nor is this all. Even women, he adds, feel
qualified to meddle in these sacred matters!

To remedy his new friend's ignorance of the Bible the Saint makes
a quick survey of the books of the Old and New Testament. Of Leviticus he has this to say: "The meaning of Leviticus is of course self-evi-
dent, although every sacrifice it describes, nay more every word it
contains, the description of Aaron's vestments and all the regulations
connected with the Levites, are symbols of things heavenly."

Paulinus was quick to take Jerome's advice to leave all and follow
Christ. He cut, rather than loosed, the hawser that prevented his vessel
from putting out to sea, and each year we celebrate his feast on the
twenty-second of June. Others, too, took Jerome's words seriously but
with less satisfactory results. The few medieval commentators who have
written about Leviticus give what Pius XII calls "a vaguely spiritual or
mystical interpretation" and stress the "symbols of things heavenly" of
which Jerome spoke. Their piously ingenious pages capture but cannot
hold our interest today.

In part this may explain why the book is so little known although
it contains some often quoted verses. There is, for instance, the law
of talion: "If a man causes injury to one of his fellow-countrymen, he
must pay for it in the same coin, making amends for broken limb with
broken limb, for eye with eye, for tooth with tooth, the loss he inflicted,
he must undergo" (24:20).

Then there are the words so carefully deciphered each year by thou-
sands of pilgrims who stand before the Liberty Bell in Independence
Hall and read: "Proclaim Liberty throughout all the Land to all the
Inhabitants thereof" (cf. 25:10). And, let us take for a final example
the text chosen for sermons at golden weddings, jubilees of ordination
or profession and during the solemnity of the Holy Year: "You shall
sound the trumpet in all the land, and you shall consecrate the fiftieth
year, and you shall proclaim release to all that dwell in your country: it
is the year of jubilee . . ." (25:9f.).

Father Robert North's monumental study of this verse contains many valuable conclusions. The word *jubilee*, we learn, comes not from the Hebrew word which means "ram's-horn" but from one which means "release." The year prescribed as the jubilee year is not the fiftieth year but the forty-ninth, the seventh sabbatical year. It was not a universally observed calendar year but was calculated individually for the limitation of debt-servitude and the restoration of alienated property. The law affirms God's ownership of all things and the subordination of particular property acquisitions to the general welfare.

In a typological sense the jubilee of Leviticus can be understood to include eternal redemption in heaven, Christ's salvific life and all "means of grace such as the sacraments and, in its way, the Holy Year." Sound interpretation, such as Father North has given, is as necessary today as it was when Jerome wrote to Paulinus.

AN EXAMPLE OF ARRESTED DEVELOPMENT

When we read the Law we must remind ourselves of a poignant subject for speculation which Monsignor Ronald Knox calls "the antecedent will of God for His chosen people." The learned Monsignor wonders what God would have made of the Jews had they corresponded perfectly to His graces instead of resisting them as so many pages of Scripture frankly show that they did. As a result of this resistance their whole history is the history of arrested development; we never see what God meant Israel to be, because Israel failed to measure up to what God intended.

For the same reason we never see all that the Law was meant to be with all its latent powers of sanctification. Surely our Lord's condemnation of the legalistic "enslavement" imposed by Scribes and Pharisees points to the fact that the Law was not meant to be a burden. Yet that was what it had come to be. All those minutious imprisoning prescriptions were not designed to be fetters but so many means intended to unite Israel in loving communion with God.

Silently, steadily, moment by moment, Israel was meant to adhere to the divine will, to live in the divine presence, to be perfectly attuned to the divine thought, in an attitude of expendability, in a surrender that was loving, total and forever.

Father Louis Bouyer points out that two psalms show the "progressive interiorization" possible to one who loved the Law and observed its precepts. Such a man could grow in "a divine intimacy, in the dialogue of word and faith, in the prayer of faith of which the psalms are

an admirable example." Of many in Israel, this surely was true but of
the people as a whole, never.

THE LAW PRAYED

In Psalm 18, the Hebrew poet contrasts the beauty of the heavens
which are the work of God the creator with the perfection of the moral
order which is the work of God the law-giver. This psalm is recited
Monday at Prime and contains this praise of the Law:

> The Lord's perfect law, how it brings the soul back to life;
> The Lord's unchangeable decrees, how they make the simple
>   learned!
> How plain are the duties the Lord enjoins, the treasure of
>   man's heart;
> How clear is the commandment the Lord gives, the enlight-
>   enment of man's eyes!

A profound meditation on the Law is found in the longest psalm of
the psalter. All 176 verses of Psalm 118 are concerned with the observance of the Mosaic Law in its eight divisions of laws, testimonies,
precepts, statutes, commandments, judgments, words and sayings. The
whole tone of the psalm is of an I-Thou relationship which should be
the goal of every soul hungering to know and serve the Lord with unfailing fidelity.

Such a soul was the Christian Jew who was the author of the epistle
of James. He believed that "living by faith" is to be equated with "keeping the Law" and he reminds the man living under the New Covenant
that "one who gazes into that perfect law which is the law of freedom,
and dwells in the sight of it, does not forget the message; he finds something to do and does it, and his way of doing it wins him a blessing"
(1:25).

Sobered by the example of "a people that failed," we must observe
"the perfect law" and guard against the stunting of our souls, fearing
every sign of life-sapping formalism, of eclectic service, of satisfaction
with appearances, of unwillingness to pay the whole price. Mediocrity
is avoided in no other way. Any inconsistency deliberately acquiesced
in between what we do and what we believe must blight and frustrate.

For this reason Søren Kierkegaard claims that *Reduplication* is the
decisive expression of the Christian life. This means to exist in what
one believes — to transform one's life in conformity with what one
objectively holds to be true. Kierkegaard complains that many philoso-

phers, in relation to the stately philosophies they have fashioned, live
in a shack nearby. "Spiritually speaking a man's thought must be the
building in which he dwells." Fervent souls are truly free for theirs is
that "freedom, spacious and unflawed, (of one) who is walled with
God."

Daily in the invitatory of Matins recur the words: "Today if you
shall hear His voice, harden not your hearts, as your fathers did in
the wilderness." Generous acceptance of the divine invitations, fidelity
in the loving observance of all His laws, a refusal to compromise with
self, will make it possible for the Lord some day to lead us into His own
dwelling place.

A TUTOR BRINGING US TO CHRIST

Before we close the book of Leviticus one final problem must be faced.
In what sense did St. Paul want us to think of the Law as "a tutor
bringing us to Christ"? What is the real meaning of so much insistence
on "the clean and the unclean"? The answer to these questions is the
beautiful one of an all-holy God wishing to make holy those whom He
loves. Many texts make this clear: "I am Yahweh who makes you
holy" (20:8). Again: "Be holy because I am holy" (9:45). And: "I
shall sanctify myself in those who draw near me" (10:3).

God's holiness and His will to make men holy explain the careful
rules governing the purity of the priest-offerer, the loyal observance
of ritual and the choice of a victim without blemish. Only in this way
could men be prepared for the perfection of the true sacrifice in which
the spotless Lamb of God takes away the sins of the world. God's holiness and His will to make men holy explain the necessity of a people
set apart from all other peoples and united to one another and to God
by a strict moral and liturgical code. Only in this way could men be prepared for the Church in which all its members are united to each other
and to God in work and worship. God's holiness and His will to make
men holy explain the need felt by every generous soul to make the
perfect offering of all that one has and will ever be. As Mother Janet
Erskine says: "The best, the first, the dearest — all for Thee."

In truth dare we aspire so high? With grace we know all things are
possible. And St. John (1:17) adds for our comfort: "Through Moses
the Law was given us; through Jesus Christ grace came to us, and
truth"!

THE BOOK OF NUMBERS

IN OUR Bibles the fourth book of the Pentateuch is called Numbers, a translation of the title found in the Greek Septuagint. In modern editions of the Hebrew Bible it is called, *In the Wilderness*, and in older manuscripts it was known as, *And Yahweh Spoke*.

These three titles, each in its own way, can unlock for us part of the meaning of a book that tells the story of the Israelites during their years in the desert after they left Egypt and before they entered the Promised Land. In the wilderness the descendants of the twelve sons of Jacob had to pattern their lives in a manner befitting a people God had chosen in a special way to be His own, to protect themselves against their enemies, to learn to hear and heed His word. Three tasks which in our passage through the world are also ours.

The *Oxford English Dictionary* lists eighteen different ways in which the word *number* may be used. Not all of these are to be found in the fourth book of the Bible but in it so many examples do occur of adding, counting, calculating, computing, enumerating, listing, measuring, organizing, reckoning, tallying and weighing that the Greek translator's choice of his title seems well justified.

LOVE OF PRECISION

No doubt the most obvious reason for his choice of this title was the census the Israelites made shortly after they left Egypt, described at the beginning of the book (1–4); and there is a second account of a census

33

made of all the fighting men, when they stood in the plain of Moab, across the Jordan opposite Jericho, shortly before the death of Moses (26).

In other chapters the number-conscious writer gives many examples of his love for precision. He tells us: the exact sum of covered wagons and oxen to be offered by the chieftains when the tabernacle was to be hallowed (7); the measure to be observed in the making of welcome-offerings, bloodless-offerings and burnt-sacrifice (15); the quantities of yearling lambs, bull-calves, bushels of flour, libations of wine, etc., to be presented to the Lord at each great feast (28–29); the muster of men selected to wreak vengeance on the Madianites and the enumeration of every category of booty seized when the Madianites were vanquished (31); the dimensions of the cities and the precincts to be set apart for the Levites when they reached the Promised Land (35).

A similar concern for exactitude is evident in the specifications given as to the length of the Levites' term of service (4:3), the membership of the advisory committee of the elders of Israel chosen to share Moses' prophetic office (11:16), the duration of Mary's exclusion from camp (12:15), the size of the rebel faction led by Core (16:2), the number of those smitten by divine justice for this revolt (16:49), the period of purification required by men defiled (19:11), the time and conditions for valid oaths and vows (30:15).

A concern about number, quantity and size is matched by a power of methodical organization. Details of life in the wilderness are foreseen, problems are solved, difficulties are met with practical rules and suitable regulations. The rights of each tribe are recognized: the good of the whole is safeguarded. Larger tribes are given larger camping grounds and allotted space closer to the sanctuary. When a fluctuation in tribal membership is revealed in the second census, a corresponding adjustment is made: the increase in the number of the fighting men of Juda assures them of an increase in territory assigned across the Jordan, while the decrease observable in Ruben and Ephraim diminishes the holdings that are to be theirs.

CONCERN FOR CLASSIFICATION

A concern for neat and orderly classifications is evident in the chapters devoted to the ecclesiastical hierarchy. Ever since the night that God had spared the Israelites' first-born sons when the Angel of death had struck all the other first-born in the land of Egypt, the eldest son in every Israelite family had been dedicated to God's service.

Now it was decreed that instead of the first-born son of every family of every tribe, all the males of one tribe should belong in a special way to God and be devoted to His service. The tribe of Levi was the one divinely chosen. To this tribe Moses belonged. Aaron, his older brother, was named high priest. Aaron's sons and their descendants were chosen to be priests and to spend their lives in God's service. They were to be assisted by the Levites, the descendants of Levi by other branches of the family.

Lest the older custom be forgotten, with its beautiful recognition that God is the great Life-giver and Liberator, it was decreed that every first-born son had to be offered to God and redeemed by the payment of a fixed sum: a fact on which we meditate in the fourth joyful mystery and which is beautifully enshrined in the liturgy of the feast of the Presentation when "Jesus Christ, the faithful witness, first-born of the living and the dead, the ruler over all earthly kings" was offered to His Father.

The Levites were solemnly dedicated by Moses on Mount Sinai and prepared for their sacred duties. They were set apart to assist the priests: to move the tabernacle from camp to camp, to guard the sacred vessels, to flay victims offered in sacrifice, to prepare the show bread, to take part in the singing. Since they belong to God, He alone was their portion and inheritance. No land of their own was promised them in Canaan, but enclaves in the midst of every tribe were assigned for their use, and all Israel was told to pay tithes to the men who represented them before the Lord (18:24).

THE VOW OF THE NAZARITES

The Nazarites were another dedicated group to whom special attention is paid in this book. They were men who elected to give God special honor. They incurred special obligations for a limited time or for life.

They promised not to take intoxicating beverages, cut their hair or mourn the dead. Nazarites were long held in great respect: in New Testament days St. John the Baptist, St. James the Less, St. Paul were, for a time, consecrated to God according to the laws laid down in the book of Numbers. At the close of the temporary vow, the Nazarites had to make a triple sacrifice: a sin offering (to expiate possible transgressions of the Law), a burnt offering (to express an ardent desire to honor God by signal service), a thank offering (to show gratitude for the completion of this period of dedication).

In these many ways the word *numbers* seems well chosen to be the title of this book. But it does not open to us all the lessons that the book contains.

IN THE WILDERNESS

Another insight can be gained by considering the aptness of one of
its Hebrew titles, *In the Wilderness*. The book contains the story of the
Israelites from the last days they spent at the foot of Mount Sinai until
they stood within sight of the Promised Land, forty years after their
fathers had left Egypt. This story is composed of historical incidents,
interspersed with bits of legislation.

The facts fall neatly into three sections corresponding to the three
regions in which the Israelites made their home: in the wilderness of
Sinai in the south (1:1–10:10), in the wilderness of Pharan in the
north (10:11–22:1), in the desolate plains of Moab which slope from
the highlands to the Jordan where it flows into the Dead Sea (22:2–
36:13).

What happened during these years in the wilderness? At the foot of
Mount Sinai, preparations were made for the journey toward the Promised Land, the tabernacle was hallowed, the Passover celebrated and
when the cloud that overshadowed the tabernacle moved, the Israelites
set out, never encamping until it settled over their next stopping place.

God's plans did not meet with Israel's approval. When they reached
the wilderness of Pharan they began to assail the Lord with their complaints. "If we had but meat to feed on! they said. How well we remember the fish that Egypt afforded without stint, the cucumbers, the mel-
ons, the leeks and onions and garlic! Our hearts faint within us, as we
look round and nothing but manna meets our eyes" (11:5–7).

The comment made by St. John of the Cross on this incident deserves
our attention:

Oh, would that spiritual persons knew how they are losing
the good things of the Spirit, abundantly furnished, because they will not
raise up their desires above trifles, and how they might have the sweetness of
all things in the pure food of the Spirit if they would only forego them. The
people of Israel perceived not the sweetness of every taste in the manna
because they would not limit their desires to it alone. The sweetness and
strength of the manna was not for them, not because it was not there, but
because they longed for other meats (*Ascent* 1:5).

The conclusion to the story is starkly recorded. It, too, carries a
lesson that St. Augustine claims few men ever learn. In his *Confessions*
he acknowledges that he had to strive daily against greediness in food
and drink and he asks: "Who is he, Lord, that is not carried somewhat
beyond the limits of the necessary? If such a man there be, he is great."

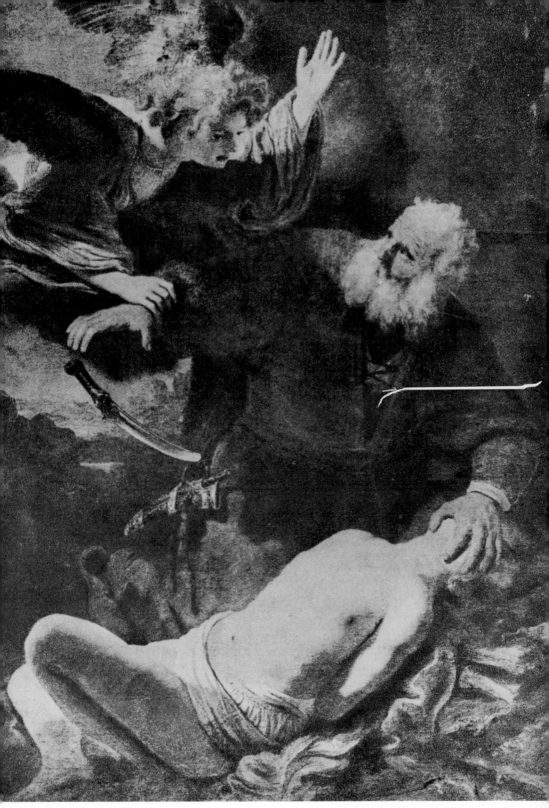

THE SACRIFICE OF ABRAHAM, Rembrandt, 1635, Leningrad, Hermitage, p. 9.

REBECCA AND ELIEZAR. German woodcut, p. 11.

JOSEPH'S MEETING WITH HIS BROTHERS, Peter Cornelius, 1815, Rome, Casa Bartholdy, p. 1:

JACOB WRESTLING WITH THE ANGEL,
Rembrandt, Berlin, Kaiser, Friedrich Museum, p. 6.

Of this greatness the Israelites had no part that day, for in answer to their complaints

            the Lord sent a wind that brought a flight of quails over the sea . . . quails that hovered two feet above the ground. All that day and that night and the next day the Israelites busied themselves gathering in quails. . . . The supply had not yet begun to fail, when suddenly a grievous plague fell on them, sentence of the divine anger they had provoked; and the place was called ever after, The Graves of Greed, from the men that lay buried there whose greed was their undoing (12:31–34).

But the troubles of the Israelites were not yet over. Soon after, Moses sent twelve spies to reconnoitre the land beyond the Jordan to which God was leading them: the minority report was made by Josue, who was to be Moses' successor, and Caleb, the representative of the tribe of Juda: "The land is fertile; let us advance; we can make it ours!" The majority report was a dismal admission of craven fear and cowardly inferiority.

Do these two reports point to two types of souls? Or to the same soul in moments when all trust is placed in God, and in moments when fear replaces trust? God's verdict leaves us in no doubt as to His preference. Because the Israelites adopted the opinion of the majority they were condemned to wander for forty more years. Not they, but their children, would enter the land from which they were barred because of their mistrust.

THEIR HISTORY IS OUR LIFE

There is a parable in these long years of wandering that is not hard to apply. Take a map of the wilderness, trace on it the Israelites' long slow journey. Had God so directed, in a few weeks time they might have entered the Promised Land. Instead He willed them to wait, to move when the cloud lifted, to battle with unpleasant neighbors, to accept life under distasteful conditions until the day of His choosing when they could cross the Jordan and reach their home. Monsignor Ronald Knox was reminded by this that in all our lives death is very near:

            A short illness or a sudden accident may carry us off at any moment. Our life is not a stately progress towards death; it is a drifting up and down, up and down, in the wilderness of this unsubstantial world, waiting for the moment when the cloud will lift for the last time, and death will come.

This will be at the moment ordained by God. Then all these years of sufferings patiently borne, disappointments lovingly accepted, joys gratefully received will be seen in their true light, the cloud will lift for the last time and we will find ourselves in our true home.

AND YAHWEH SPOKE

In the midst of these years of wandering the Lord gave many laws to His people. But it is not to these far-off laws that we will now apply the older Hebrew title of the book: *And Yahweh Spoke*. Rather we will ask ourselves what were the great truths divinely taught when the Lord spoke to His people in the wilderness.

The years between the moment the Israelites stood on the shores of the Red Sea and the moment when they stood on the banks of the Jordan are obviously the most decisive period in the history of Israel. It is to the Old Law what the lifetime of Jesus is to the New. No other period was marked by so many miracles, so many divine interventions, so many manifestations of the divine presence.

This period was annually commemorated in the Israelite liturgy. The old agrarian feasts were transformed into memorial celebrations: the springtime feast of the first barley harvest was associated with the Passover, the feast of unleavened bread, and the miraculous departure from Egypt; the early summer feast of the wheat harvest was associated with Pentecost and the promulgation of the Law on Mount Sinai fifty days after the crossing of the Red Sea; and the autumn vineyard feast became the feast of Tabernacles commemorating the outdoor life of the Israelites during these forty years.

The great prophets of Israel looked on this period as an ideal age when God was fashioning His people and teaching them that their love must be for Him alone. He was not only invisible, transcendent and supreme but the God of their fathers, who had brought them out of Egypt, who guided them with tender love. The psalmist's words are true of the days of the exodus and of today: "The Lord is my Shepherd: how can I lack anything? He gives me a resting place where there is pasture, and leads me out by cool waters, to make me live anew. Hurt I fear none while Thou art with me" (23:1–4).

The book of Wisdom invites us to look deeper into the meaning of these divine gifts: the food He provided mattered less than the words He spoke. The Israelites were meant "to learn that man lives, not by the ripening of crops, but by Thy word, ever protecting the souls that trust in Thee" (17:26).

GOD'S CONTINUING LOVE

It is surprising that a book so meaningful seldom appears in our liturgy. On Friday in the third week of Lent allusion is made to the water that

Moses drew for his people from a rock (21:11). On the feast of the Purification, an antiphon recalls the star that rose out of Jacob (24:17). On the feast of the Exaltation of the Cross, a breviary lesson commemorates the brazen serpent that brought healing when Moses held it up for all to see (21:1–9). In the votive Mass to be said in time of widespread epidemic, there is a reference to the high priest who stood between the living and the dead, holding high a golden censer so that the divinely imposed affliction might cease (16:48). In the rite of ordination the seventy elders chosen by Moses are held up as models to those about to be ordained (11:25).

Nor are there many references to the book of Numbers in other parts of the Bible. An examination of some of these passages serves as an excellent introduction to the book and shows its composite nature. Mosaic in authorship like the other books of the Pentateuch, the book of Numbers was revised by inspired writers in the course of centuries. Yet the book has a unity because of the insistence on God's continuing love. This is evident not only in the mathematically detailed sections, but also in the accounts of life in the wilderness and the beautiful lessons Yahweh then taught His people.

Praise of God's holy ones	Ecclus. 45:1–46:12
Infidelity in the desert	Ps. 106
The manna (11:7)	John 6:31
The fidelity of Moses (12:7)	Heb. 3:2–5
The revolt of Core (16:1–50)	Jude 11:2
The tithes (18:21–24)	Heb. 7:5
The red cow (19)	Heb. 9:13
The brazen serpent (21:4–9)	John 3:14
The story of Balaam (22–24)	2 Peter 2:15
The flock without a shepherd (27:17)	Matt. 9:36

MEASURED . . . WEIGHED . . . CALCULATED

Aristotle held the art of numbers in high esteem. To him it was one of the three theoretical sciences, ranking with theology which is the same thing as "first philosophy" and with the philosophy of nature which is usually translated by the word "physics." Men have gone far in their thinking since the days when Aristotle's pupil, Alexander, was realizing his concept of "One World"; and within the last century, numbers and philosophy have been brought together in the challenging concepts of symbolic logic of which neither the Greek philosopher nor the mathematically-minded author of the book of Numbers gives us any hint.

But the inspired writer did possess a far more valuable understanding of the beauty of wisely ordered reality than mathematics or logic alone can afford. This insight underlies his account of the years spent by the Israelites in the desert and the lessons God then taught and gives a deeper meaning to his title than his own flair for figures or his love for IBM precision. This insight may be expressed in words addressed to God in the book of Wisdom: "All that Thou doest is done in exact measure, all is nicely calculated and weighed" (Wis. 11:20).

It is this reverence for divine providence that gives dignity to the book of Numbers. In it we find a climate of thought that is serene and unshakably secure. Little children who do not know the meaning of distrust have this precious gift, as do interior souls who in hours of keenest pain have embraced the divine will, without heeding its human instruments, avoiding all introspection and idle analysis, seeking no solutions but those that are supernatural, deepening within themselves and imparting to others their conviction that God is all-good, all-wise, all-merciful.

If this is done joyfully and with a very great love, then they, too, will see that to bring them into His promised land all life's joys and sorrows have been meted out by God in exact measure; to draw souls closer to Him He has, indeed, nicely calculated and weighed all things.

THE BOOK OF DEUTERONOMY

DEUTERONOMY is the fifth book of the Jewish Law, the *Torah*. This is no dry list of legal formulae, no dull enumeration of prohibitions and punishments but earnest, persuasive appeals to give glad and loyal service to the Lord. These pleas are presented in the form of three discourses. Time and place are carefully indicated for these warmly personal addresses which are said to have been delivered by Moses to the Chosen People in the land of Moab, beyond the Jordan, not long before he died. History, homily and liturgy are happily combined in these richly theological expositions of the Law which are followed by an appendix describing the last words and last days of Israel's lawgiver. Moses' final discourse to his people closes with this solemn exhortation:

Take to heart all the warning which I have now given you and which you must impress on your children, that you may carry out carefully every word of this law. For this is no trivial matter for you; rather it means your very life, since it is by this means that you are to enjoy a long life on the land which you will cross the Jordan to occupy (28:46f).

It is the figure of Moses and his doctrine of "faithful service rewarded" that gives unity to this book which is composed of a multitude of disparate elements and for whose composition no completely satisfactory date or pattern has been proposed. It would seem that its

41

present form is the result of a long period of oral transmission and a succession of editors but its basic principles are those of the thirteenth century lawgiver and these are offered in a form well calculated to renew the fervor of the people of God of every age as they once did the subjects of King Josias in seventh-century Judea.

The scene is described in the fourth book of Kings, chapters 22 and 23 (cf. 2 Par. 34). Josias was a model sovereign who walked steadfastly in the footsteps of David, deviating neither to left or right, always doing what was right in the eyes of the Lord. So in the eighteenth year of his reign (621), wishing to renew and strengthen the zeal of his people for the Law of the Lord, he assembled them in the temple and bade them listen to "the words of the book of the covenant." The reform was immediate, if not lasting: foreign cults were banned, the law was once more observed in all its purity. The pasch was observed as never before. The "book" so closely connected with the king's strict enforcement of the law which had been recently discovered in the temple was probably some part of Deuteronomy, that is, "a second law," and most likely included the massive sections of legislation known as the Deuteronomic code (12–26). This "second law" (to borrow the name the Greeks chose as a title for this book when they translated it from the Hebrew and placed it in the Septuagint) is an amplified version with additional historical material of the legislation recorded in the book of Exodus (20–23). It is more detailed than the "first law" which was made on Mount Sinai shortly after the Israelites left Egypt, more specific about the blessings God reserves for those who faithfully follow Him no matter what the cost:

If only thou wilt be true to the commandments of the Lord thy God, and follow the paths He has chosen, He will fulfill His promise, and make thee a people set apart for Himself. The Lord will make thee rich in all good things; fruitful thy own race; fruitful thy cattle; fruitful this land His promised gift to thy fathers. . . . all this, if thou wilt obey the commandments of the Lord" (28:9, 13).

ECHOES IN THE OLD TESTAMENT

These pure and profound truths are not only at the heart of the reforms of Josias: the lessons of Deuteronomy are to be found in many of the books of sacred Scripture. In fact they seem to have inaugurated a literary movement destined to waken in men's hearts a love for the Lord and His law which lasted down to New Testament days and does much to help us to understand the climate of thought in the early Church. The theme of "one God, one sanctuary" was to become the touchstone of orthodoxy for the author of the fourth book of Kings. The same spirit pervades the books of Paralipomena, where fidelity to the covenant is stressed and the kings of Juda are judged according to the precepts of Deuteronomy. In Jeremias, too, we find its teaching about "circumcision of heart" and its plea for a religion that is inward and heart-true. Its denunciation of idolatry and its pledge of ultimate victory for a purified Israel resemble the teaching of the last chapters of Isaias. While in Ezechiel, references to the sword of justice, the day of vengeance and the annihilation of pagan foes are echoes of the vigorous didactic poem in Deuteronomy which is known as the "Canticle of Moses."

Perhaps the most significant of all these influences is to be found in those pages of the Old Testament in which the Law is held up for reverent homage. This is especially clear in many of the psalms. Each one of the 176 verses of psalm 118 could be cited to illustrate the relationship between God and man, and the perfection of God's Law which is so strongly inculcated in the last book of the Pentateuch.

ECHOES IN THE NEW TESTAMENT

Father R.A.F. MacKenzie, S.J., in a study made recently of messianism in Deuteronomy, shows that a casual reading of the book reveals little that refers directly to the life and mission of the Messias although the New Testament itself contains many allusions to its pages. How to reconcile this anomaly? The Acts of the Apostles show that the early Christian community found in Deuteronomy proofs of God's love for His people in the past, and promises of greater blessings to be communicated to the true Israel by a great prophet, a second Moses. This "realized eschatology" is one of the great legacies of the book. Saint Peter encouraged the Christians to consider themselves this holy and faithful Israel (Acts 3:22). Saint Stephen, too, interprets passages of Deuteronomy as fulfilled in the early Church (7:37). Further links like this can easily be found not only in the Acts but also in the Gospels. Although the prophecy of Moses that "The Lord thy God will raise up to thee a prophet of thy nation and of thy brethren like unto me" is to be understood as a collective figure and was fulfilled in such men as Samuel, Elias, Eliseus and their successors; Saint John is obviously referring to this ideal prophet when he quotes the words of the crowd after the multiplication of loaves: "This is indeed the prophet who is to come into the world" (6:14). On the last day of the feast of the Tabernacles, the crowd again expressed the same thought, after hearing Jesus speak: "This man must surely be the prophet" (7:40).

Saint Matthew develops another theme from Deuteronomy when he shows that Christ, the perfect Israel, fulfills the obligations that the ancient Israel was unable fully to meet (cf. Matt. 4:1–11). In words as well as in works are analogies between the Gospels and Deuteronomy to be found. Christ's great commandment: "Thou shalt love the Lord thy God with thy whole heart, and with thy whole soul, and with thy whole mind" (Matt. 22:37), a commandment on which, He adds, all the other commandments depend, and which Saint Paul explains is their synthesis (Rom. 13:8f) is found to be formulated in Deuteronomy's great profession of faith:

Listen then, O Israel; there is no Lord but the Lord thy God, thou shalt love the Lord thy God with the love of thy whole heart, and thy whole strength. The commands I give thee this day must be written on thy heart, so that thou canst teach them to thy sons, and keep them in mind continually, at home and on thy travels, sleeping and waking; ever close to thy hand as a signet ring, ever moving up and down before thy eyes; the legend thou dost inscribe on door and gatepost" (6:4–9).

The first word of this passage, *Shema* (*Listen!*), has given its name to the prayer recited by devout Jews morning and evening from Old Testament days to the present. Gradually it became customary to interpret the words literally, so certain passages from the Torah (Deut. 6:4–9; 11:13–21; Ex. 13:1–10, 11–16) were copied on parchment, enclosed in small leather cases and worn on the left arm and forehead. These prayer-bands were called *phylacteries* by the Greeks. Jesus censured the Pharisees for their exaggerated concern about the externals of worship, blaming them for making the cases and bands of their phylacteries ostentatiously broad (Matt. 23:5).

CELEBRATE THE PASCH

Deuteronomy gave the Chosen People not only formulae for prayer but also explicit instructions about the great feasts and the reasons for their celebration. Fear men must, so great is the Lord's majesty but hope should grow strong in every heart, so powerful are His promises, and love is seen to be man's only adequate response to so tender and jealous a love. The author does more than lay down precepts; he explains the moral purpose of the Law with the moving rhetoric of great oratory. He pleads with his hearers to celebrate the great feasts which commemorate God's goodness to their race. Of the pasch he says: Mark well that first spring month when the crops are yet green; it is time to celebrate the pasch in the Lord's honour. In that month, at dead of night, the Lord thy God rescued thee from Egypt. In the place which the Lord thy God has chosen for the sanctuary of His name, flock and herd alike must provide their paschal victims. . . . never as long as thou livest shall the manner of thy departure from Egypt be forgotten (16:1–3).

GIVE THANKS TO THE LORD

God's protecting love for His people is a theme that recurs in many places in Deuteronomy. Some of these passages have been introduced into the liturgy of the Church. Reference is made in spring and summer Ember day Masses to the goodness of God who has brought His people into a land flowing with milk and honey, and invited them to feast on all the good things He has given. But nowhere is the spirit of this book more perfectly presented than in the Easter vigil service which is the solemn memorial of the central mystery of our redemption. In it the Church acknowledges the lessons it has learned "through thy holy servant Moses"; whole chapters from Deuteronomy provide beautiful commentaries on phrases from the liturgy of the Light Service and the Baptismal Service.

This is the night in which Thou didst of old lead our forefathers, the children of Israel out of the land of Egypt (The Exsultet). . . . Deut. 1–4.

Grant that the whole world may become children of Abraham and enter into the heritage of Israel (Prayer after Second Reading). . . . Deut. 9–11.

Grant them Thy strength to root out the tangle of briars and thorns, and to bring forth worthy fruit in abundance (Prayer after Third Reading). . . . Deut. 27–28.

In those days: Moses wrote this song and taught it to the Israelites (Fourth Reading). . . . Deut. 31–32.

While they thereby proclaimed Thy law we too were being instructed (Prayer after Fourth Reading). . . . Deut. 33–34.

And in the Eucharistic Service the gradual verses sum up the teaching of the "second law":

Give thanks to the Lord, for He is good; for His mercy endures forever. . . . Steadfast is His kindness towards us, and the fidelity of the Lord endures forever.

WHY . . . WHAT . . . WHICH

To list these influences of Deuteronomy on the books of the Old and New Testament is to give no true picture of the book itself. This entails a voyage of discovery each one best makes alone. For those who like method even in their literary travels, the following questions may prove helpful:

1. Why were the men who left Egypt condemned to wander for forty years in the desert? (1:19–40)
2. What proofs of His love did God give His people? (4:32–40)
3. Which commandments did He enjoin? (5:1–33)
4. Explain the Law of One Sanctuary. (12:1–31)
5. How were the people to observe the feast of the Passover, the feast of Weeks and the feast of Booths? (16:1–17)
6. In what way were the people told to thank God? (26:1–19)
7. When did Moses name Josue to be his successor? (31:1–8)
8. Summarize the doctrine in the spirited "Canticle of Moses." (32:1–43)
9. How did Moses bless the twelve tribes? (33:1–29)
10. Describe the death and burial of Moses. (34:1–12)

IN CHRIST SUFFERING AND CHRIST TRIUMPHANT

So deeply spiritual a book with its lessons on man's unquestioning service and God's unfailing rewards has in every age supplied texts for sermons and subjects for prayer. Let us consider two texts that appealed to St. John of the Cross and one that meant much to his co-worker St. Teresa. The first is found at the beginning of the book in a summary of God's goodness to His people. Here Moses recalls that the Lord, who had spoken from the heart of flaming fire on the summit of the mountain which rose out of thick darkness, clouds and mist, is "a fire that burns all before it and He loves thee with a jealous love" (4:24). The second is found in the canticle in which Moses exalts the power of the God of Israel, the one, true God and laments Israel's failure to respond: "A people so well loved! and now, pampered, they would throw off the yoke. Pampered, full-fed, swollen with pride, they forsook their divine creator, revolted against their deliverer" (32:15).

These two texts have been beautifully treated by Saint John of the Cross. Several times he reminds his readers that the Lord is "a consuming fire." This fire, he teaches, is the fire of charity, and in it we are united to God. Faith kindles this divine fire in the soul, and makes us one with God in Christ suffering and Christ triumphant, because the same flame that in pain destroys our selfishness, in glory rewards our love.

In his commentary on the first stanza of "The Living Flame of Love" the saint explains that "the same fire of love which afterwards is united with the soul and glorifies it is that which aforetime assailed it in order to purify. . . . and in this purgatorial state the flame is not bright but dark. Neither is it sweet but grievous; for although at times it kindles within it the warmth of love, this is accompanied by torment and affliction."

But a time will come, the saintly Carmelite promises, when the divine flame will consume and give no pain. For the soul that has attained to perfect love is conformed so sweetly to God that God becomes not only a consuming but "a consummating and a renewing fire."

PAMPERED, FULL-FED, SWOLLEN WITH PRIDE

The second quotation from Deuteronomy provided the saint with an unpleasant text for his description of the four evils that befall souls whose exclusive delight is in the world's goods. "Pampered, full-fed, swollen with pride, they forsook their divine creator, revolted against their deliverer." "Pampered" souls, he warns, whose desires for foolish things are unbridled, no matter how high their holiness, how keen their understanding, will find their minds blunted and their vision of the things of God obscured as in a mist. This is the first privative evil. The second is experienced by "full-fed" souls who surfeit themselves with imperfections, vanities and follies and who concern themselves with holy practices only through formality or under compulsion. The third evil follows fast upon the second, for these souls who have grown lax in love soon forsake their Creator. Their final failure is to reverse the divine order, to place temporal things above eternal, and to consider the present value of each object rather than its divine worth and reward.

THE THIRD SPIRITUAL ALPHABET

One of the treasures of the Carmelites of Avila is a sixteenth century copy of Fray Francisco de Osuna's *Third Spiritual Alphabet*. This book once belonged to Saint Teresa. It was given to her by her uncle at a critical moment in her spiritual life and she tells in her autobiography that from the moment that she took it as her guide she made rapid progress in the ways of prayer. The author was a saintly son of Saint Francis; he was named to govern the newly discovered American provinces of his order but never crossed the seas to the new world, devoting himself to the needs of the Church in Spain. He is the author of six books, each bearing as title the word *Alphabet*. This was a literary device popular in his day based on the pattern of the Lamentations of

Jeremias. Each book has twenty-six chapters and each chapter begins with a different letter of the alphabet.

Saint Teresa studied Osuna's *Third Alphabet* with absorbing attention. Visitors to the Avila Convent who have examined the yellow pages she dearly loved find that she filled their margins with little hearts, crosses and other signs to indicate her favorite sentences. Sometimes she underlined whole passages in which the soul is told how to prepare for those things which no man can teach but only God.

THE MOST NEEDFUL SCRIPTURE

It is Osuna's sixteenth chapter that is of greatest interest to us here. It has for title: "The Letter R. Refer all things to love and from all things draw love." After praising love and showing the value of love in the soul's prayer life, Osuna says that sacred Scripture is the answer to the question: "What is the chief source from which we may draw love?" Sacred Scripture, he reasons, is inspired by the Holy Ghost who is love, and so it must contain no little bit of that precious quality. He illustrates his point with some beautiful paragraphs on the Ten Commandments (5:2–3) which are, he says, "the most needful Scripture," explaining that if we interpret the divine law by the perfection of love, we shall discover that in breaking the first commandment the soul, in a way, is guilty of breaking them all. For he who does not love God with all his heart and strength and more than all other things takes His Name in vain, for in vain does man bear the name of Christian if he does not wholly love God. Nor does he know how to keep sacred the Lord's day since God is honored by joy and true repose of the soul in Him who is our infinite Good. Not to love God is to dishonor one's father and mother, who can have no higher praise than to call into being a creature able to love and possess God. The man who does not love God not only slays his own soul but makes himself unworthy of temporal life which is given us for the service of the divine majesty. The man who does not love God is an arrant thief. God made our hearts for Himself. He gave His Heart to us. To give our hearts to another is to take from God what belongs to Him. For a baptized soul to love a creature more than God is spiritual adultery because in baptism the soul was espoused to Him. To fail in love is to bear false witness, for such a man seems to be a Christian but is in fact a trickster, for he is not what he seems. Finally against the last two commandments the unloving soul also offends because he covets those things to which he has no claim and which he cannot take with him into the world to come.

On the other hand if we accustom ourselves to refer all things to love and to derive love from all things, we will find that we will keep the first commandment and that this is the fulfillment of the whole law. Saint Teresa did not underscore this ingenious passage in *The Third Alphabet* but in her own writings there is abundant evidence that she had made its teaching her own. The pre-eminence of love is stressed in all her counsels and she often taught the same lesson to her nuns in these direct words: "God does not want our deeds but He does want the love that prompts them."

FRIEND OF GOD

Moses, the mighty figure whose last days are recorded in the book of Deuteronomy, is presented as the leader, the law-giver, the friend of God, the precursor of Christ. No other prophet was his equal, worked greater miracles, overcame greater foes, spoke more familiarly with the Lord.

The Sistine Chapel is a tribute in line and colour, light and shadow expressing men's high esteem for this fearless and very human hero of the Exodus. On the left wall great Renaissance painters, Perugino, Signorelli, Botticelli, have depicted scenes from his life; on the right wall are corresponding scenes from the life of Christ, so that we may turn from the Old Law to the New, from the type to the anti-type. In giving us this lesson the artists were extolling the virtues of one held up for their veneration by both Latin Fathers and Greek.

Saint Augustine gratefully acknowledges his pre-eminence in these words: "Moses, the servant of the living God . . . is humble when he refuses so great a mission, submissive when he accepts it, faithful when he carries it out, intrepid when he completes it. He is assiduous in governing his people, zealous in correcting them, ardent in loving them, patient in putting up with them. When God consults him, he intercedes for them; when God is angry with them, he interposes himself. . . . It is on the evidence offered us by God that we love Moses His servant, that we admire him, that we imitate him as much as we can, that we acknowledge how far he surpasses us in every way."

Saint Gregory of Nyssa at the end of the life-story of Moses does not hesitate to say that if we would be perfect we must take this friend of God as our model, imitating his fear of God, his hope, his love. "Now is the moment to turn towards this model and to express in your own life the spiritual meaning of these historic events so that God will recognize you as His friend and this you will be in truth. For true perfection consists not in turning away from a sinful life through fear of punishment, like a slave; nor of doing good through hope of reward, trafficking in virtue like a selfish, calculating man; but hoping beyond the hope of all the good things promised, fearing only the loss of our friendship with God, and esteeming only one thing honorable and worthy of our love, namely to be God's friend — this I believe is perfection. . . ."

THIS IS THE DAY THE LORD HAS MADE

Holy fear, firm hope, love proved by pain are the virtues the brilliant bishop of Nyssa would have us practice and he is right in thinking that of these virtues Moses has left us an example, for his life was spent in journeying towards the Promised Land. Let us then hasten onward like a runner pressing towards the goal, unmindful of what is behind, stretching forward to the good things God has in store for those who love Him.

Nor need we wonder what we had best do. A greater than Moses has gone before us in the way. If we have listened to His words and walked with Him in His sufferings then we have understood. In the words of Deuteronomy He tells us that what He asks of us is within the power of every soul of good will:

It is not above thy reach, it is not beyond thy compass, this duty which I am now enjoining upon thee. It is not a secret laid up in heaven, that thou must needs find someone to scale heaven and bring it down to thee before thou canst hear what it is, and obey it. It is not an art practised far overseas, that thou must wait for someone to go voyaging and bring it back to thee before thou canst learn to live by it. No, this message of Mine is close to thy side; it rises to thy lips; it is printed on thy memory; thou hast only to fulfill it (30:17–20).

To this earnest plea a life of generous service is our best response.

THE BOOK OF JOSUE

THE book of Josue answers the question: How did the Israelites take possession of the Promised Land? The story begins on the eastern side of the Jordan forty years after they had escaped from the bondage of Egypt. Moses, God's friend and faithful servant, had guided his people through the desert, from the shores of the Red Sea to the banks of the Jordan. God had given them every proof of His love and Moses had taught them by word and example.

One failure alone seems to mar his record (Deut. 3:25). When he pleaded to be allowed to enter the Promised Land, he was refused. From one so high in office, so eminent in sanctity, so rich in grace, a fault publicly committed must be signally atoned. Even pagans knew this. Plato could write: "When we break away from order through some fault, we can return to order only through suffering." Moses understood. Humbly he submitted. Sin — any sin — assumes a gravity in the eyes of the soul who has learned something of God's infinite purity; then pain, the price of reparation, is paid gratefully and with love.

Moses asked God to name a successor. Josue was chosen. Before all the people Moses was told to lay his hands on Josue, the external rite signifying the transference of power, and "to give him a part of his glory," that is, to tell the people that they must now obey the man who so long had stood loyally at his side.

From the wooded slopes of Mount Nebo, the traveler can see to the

51

south the shining surface of the apparently mis-named Dead Sea, at his feet the tortuous bed of the Jordan which twists and turns as if reluctant to reach its goal, and to the west and to the north as far as the eye can reach stretch the green hills and golden fields of Palestine. Here Moses died.

BEGINNING WITH MOSES AND ALL THE PROPHETS

To ask ourselves which incident of our Lord's life we would choose to witness, were the privilege ours, is a question with many answers. But most students of sacred Scripture must, at one time or another, have longed to have traveled along the road from Jerusalem to Emmaus that first Easter Sunday afternoon when the courteous Stranger, after gently rebuking His sad-faced, slow-hearted, unbelieving companions, spoke to them of Moses and the whole line of the prophets, explaining the words these men had used of Himself.

With burning hearts, we think, we too would have begged Him to stay with us when He made as if to go further, and we would have rejoiced when He agreed to remain for the breaking of bread.

Josue, surely, was one of the prophets "made plain" to the disciples that spring day, because in the Hebrew bible, which is divided differently than ours, Josue is the first of the "ancient prophets." This division may originally have been determined by the synagogal reading of the inspired text. The *Law* contained the first five books of Moses; the *Prophets* contained the books of Josue, Judges, Kings, Isaias, Jeremias, Ezechiel and the minor prophets; while all the other Old Testament books are known as the *Writings*.

Josue, it may be objected, is a book of history, why list it as prophetical? Briefly the reason is this: the Hebrews considered history and its recording to be prophetic because the prophet is one who gives men God's creative word. History is also prophetic in another sense. It is the coming true of God's creative plan. It is the fulfilment of the divine promises. This is seen in the book of Josue.

Part of God's great promise to Abraham was about to be fulfilled. To the patriarch He had said: "I will give to you and to your descendants the land of your repose, all the land of Canaan for a perpetual possession and I will be their God" (Gen. 17:8). It is the entrance of the Israelites into this "perpetual possession" that is described in the first twelve chapters; the division of the land and the closing years of Josue are described in the second half of the book. The anonymous author continues the story begun in Deuteronomy. He bases his narrative on older documents. Archaeologists busy at Bethel, Lachish and Tell Beit Mirsim have confirmed many of his facts.

TAKE COURAGE . . . I AM WITH YOU

Who was this man who was chosen to succeed Moses? His name had once been Osee (which means in Hebrew: "salvation"), but Moses had changed it to Josue (which means "the Lord is salvation"). He was the first of twenty-three men in the Bible who were to bear some form of this name which was told by the angel to Mary and to Joseph, and by which we are saved.

He was a man of God, of whom St. Jerome dared to write: "Josue resembled Jesus in deeds as well as in name." He had led an untried army against the Amalecites while Moses prayed with outstretched arms for victory. After the conclusion of the covenant, he had accompanied Moses to the top of Mount Sinai when "the Lord spoke to Moses" just as He was later to speak to Josue.

Perhaps the most significant of the many incidents in which he played an important part was his return from a secret survey of the land God had chosen for the Israelites. Twelve men made up the expedition. Josue represented the tribe of Ephraim. Their instructions were explicit: View the land. Notice if the people are strong or weak, few or many. Report on the nature of the soil, the fortifications of the cities, the products of the fields. Be of good courage and return with some samples of what grows there.

Forty days later the spies were back. Their report began favorably enough, beyond a doubt the Lord had led them to a land of blessings; as proof they pointed to a cluster of grapes so large that two men carried it on a lever from shoulder to shoulder. Then came the conclusion that was unworthy of men whose trust should have been in the Lord. "No, we are not able to go up to this people. They are tall of stature like giants: in comparison we seemed like locusts." That night the Israelites wept. "Is it not better," they asked one another, "to return to Egypt?"

At this moment of crisis Josue and Caleb, his companion, gave a minority report. To speak at all required courage: to speak as they did required what is finer than courage — trust in God. "The land which we have gone round is very good. If the Lord be favorable He will bring us into it. Be not rebellious. The Lord is with us. Fear not." Only God's manifest pleasure in their words saved the two men from being instantly stoned to death.

This incident illustrates the same lesson that our Lord is teaching today: "What is there to fear, if you are in My hands? Never doubt the goodness of My Heart, nor the love I bear you. Trust Me for everything." Sister Josefa loved these words, so should we.

Then the Lord spoke to Josue: "Arise and pass over the Jordan, you and your people with you, into the land which I will give to the children of Israel. . . . No man shall resist you all the days of your life. As I have been with Moses, so I will be with you. I will not leave you, nor forsake you. Take courage and be strong; for you shall divide by lot this land which I swore to their fathers I would deliver to them."

WHAT MEAN THESE STONES

Josue acted at once. At the Lord's command he began a singularly spectacular conquest in which he quickly overcame thirty-one kings. Ordering all twelve tribes (including the calculating sons of Ruben, Gad and Manasses who had elected to live in land they had staked out for themselves on the eastern shore) to cross the Jordan near the Dead Sea, Josue received miraculous assistance by the sudden and temporary damming of the river so that his people walked dryshod across its bed.

At this point in scholarly accounts of the invasion, learned footnotes appear explaining that God could have used natural causes to produce so favorable a situation. Experts quote an old Arab chronicler, Nuwairi, who reports that on December 7, 1267, landslides left the river bed dry for six hours. Or, they describe the effects of an earthquake in 1927, when the steep marl banks collapsed some miles above Jericho, and for twenty hours no water flowed into the Dead Sea.

More important is it to remember that whatever be the explanation, this unimpeded passage confirmed the appointment of Josue just as the crossing of the Red Sea had confirmed the appointment of Moses, and it was a pledge and token that God, who had blessed the beginning of their struggle, would give them victory at the end.

Once the Israelites had assembled on the land of promise, twelve memorial stones were erected in the middle of the river where the priests carrying the ark had halted until the travelers were happily on the other shore, and twelve stones taken from the river were carried to Galgal, where Josue ordered the law of circumcision to be observed and the passover to be celebrated. After this day the manna, which had been their principal food in the desert, ceased.

FOR OUR CORRECTION

Some interesting parallels are evident if we read with care chapters 3–5 of Josue and turn back to the corresponding incidents of the book of Exodus. The sacred writer himself seems conscious of the analogy.

The departure from Egypt and the entrance into the promised land are shown to be the work of God, who stopped the flowing Jordan as He had dried the waters of the Red Sea. Guided by the ark of the covenant, the Israelites safely followed the path traced for them across the Jordan, just as the Lord had gone before them and protected them in the desert by a pillar of cloud by day and a pillar of fire by night. Josue, like another Moses, was God's spokesman and watchful representative when they were overcome by their own weakness or assailed by doubt. Circumcision, which had prepared the people for their life lived according to God's law, is renewed for their descendants at the close of their years of wandering. And the passover was celebrated after their second miraculous passage, just as they had celebrated it in Egypt before their first.

St. Paul asks us in the epistle of Easter Sunday to consider an extension of this theme. Christ our paschal victim is sacrificed, he explains, and then he goes on to show that the passion and resurrection of Christ renew, in a spiritual way, the events of the exodus. The conclusion to the apostle's parallel is as unexpected as it is disconcerting, as demanding as it is galvanising:

> For I would not have you ignorant, brethren, that our fathers were all under the cloud, and all passed through the sea, and all were baptised in Moses, in the cloud and in the sea. And all ate the same spiritual food and all drank the same drink. . . . Yet with most of them God was not well pleased. . . . Now all these things happened to them as a type, and they were written for our correction (cf. 1 Cor. 10:1–12).

WALLS COME TUMBLING DOWN

The first towns captured were Jericho and Hai. Seven times in seven days the people circled Jericho in silence. On the last day their faith and obedience were rewarded. At the sound of the trumpets and the noise of shouting the stronghold fell. Song and story have made this one of the best known scenes in the Bible. The words of a haunting Negro spiritual acclaim the hero of the day:

Joshua fit de battle ob Jericho!
Joshua, he was best man of all.
When the lam', ram, sheep's horn begin to blow,
Trumpet begin to sound,
O Joshua commanded de chillen to shout
An' de walls come a tumblin' down!
Alleluia!

The city and its inhabitants were put under a ban; the Hebrew word for this is *herem*. In war what was under a ban belonged to the Lord because He gave the victory. The city, its inhabitants and all their possessions were destroyed. Xenophobia alone would preserve the Israelites from the baneful influence of Canaanite culture. This provisional measure was meant to save them from idolatrous contacts. Rahab the harlot and her family alone escaped. She lived in a house built up against the city walls, which recent excavations show were destroyed or deeply fissured at this time.

When St. John of the Cross was composing the eleventh chapter of the *Ascent of Mount Carmel,* "wherein it is proved that the soul that would attain to divine union should be free from desires, however small," he remembered these passages from Josue. The *herem* reminded him how great must be the soul's detachment if it is to journey on to God. *Herem,* he explained, enables us to understand how, "if a man is to enter this divine union, all that lives in his soul must die, both little and much, small and great, and that the soul must be without desire for all this and detached from it, even as though it existed not for the soul, nor the soul for it."

Whenever the opening chapter of St. Matthew's Gospel is read, the harlot of Jericho is honored as one of Christ's ancestors. This is a privilege she won, according to St. Paul, through her faith in the Lord and her willingness to shelter two spies whom Josue sent to explore the city before they invested it.

She told them that she knew the Lord of heaven had given them the land of Canaan and that the men of Jericho were full of fear because they had heard what great things God had done for the people He had chosen. She promised to help them if they in their turn would save her family when the city fell. Meanwhile the purpose of the two strangers was suspected by the authorities. She bade the spies hide on the roof and then told their pursuers that the two men had escaped through the city gate.

WHERE THEY WENT I KNOW NOT

What the two Israelites thought as they lay on the roof of Rahab's house hidden beneath the stalks of drying flax and heard their hostess' lying words, we do not know. But we do know that writers commenting on this scene have treated her very kindly. Far from flinching at the woman's outright lie, her words to the city authorities have released unsuspected reserves of chivalry and resourcefulness in exegetes of every age. They quickly focus our attention on her mercy rather than her mendacity. Cornelius a Lapide suggests that she solved her problem with faulty but well-meant dialectics. He asserts with disarming candor:

The woman did lie. This however was done not maliciously but rather through a sense of duty. Moreover hers was not a grave sin, especially since she was an unlettered pagan who had persuaded herself that in a situation like this a lie was licit, nay more, it was the honest thing to do — possibly necessary — so that she might save the lives of her guests.

Rahab's example troubled many Christians in the third and fourth centuries who asked themselves whether, in time of persecution, it was ever licit for them to lie. The Priscillians said yes. This delicate problem in moral theology was brought, like so many others, to St. Augustine, who gently but without compromise condemned the convenient errors of the noble, cultured Spanish heresiarch. A Christian, Augustine taught, must avoid a lie or confess it, never condone it. His reference to Rahab is a model of charity:

Because Rahab in Jericho gave hospitality to the men of God who came as strangers, because she endangered herself in receiving them, because she believed in their God, because she hid them as best she could, because she gave them trustworthy advice about their homeward journey — for all these reasons may she be praised by the citizens of the heavenly Jerusalem. But the fact that she lied is not proposed for imitation . . . even though God rewarded her good deeds and mercifully pardoned her bad one. . . . It was her mercy that He rewarded, not her mendacity; her good will, not her trickery; the goodness of her intention, not the evil of her invention.

GIVE GLORY TO GOD AND CONFESS

Hai, too, was under a ban. Strategists suggested that a strong force would not be needed to capture this weak city, and so two or three thousand men set out. To their surprise, their losses were heavy and they were driven back. Josue learned that their failure was due to Israel's sin. Casting lots, Achan was found to be the culprit. Josue told him to give glory to God and confess his fault. This the unhappy man did and his clear factual statement would delight a moral theologian:

"I have indeed sinned against the Lord, the God of Israel. This is what I have done: Among the spoils, I saw a beautiful Babylonian mantle, two hundred shekels of silver, and a bar of gold fifty shekels in weight; in my greed I took them. They are now hidden in the ground inside my tent, with the silver underneath" (Jos. 7:20–21).

Examination of his tent proved the truth of Achan's words. His property was burned. He and his family were stoned to death. Such summary treatment reminds us that God's laws are inexorable.

There is also another lesson to be learned. It is the lesson St. Paul taught the Galatians (6:13) when he wrote to them that "neither circumcision nor uncircumcision are of any account," and the Lord is the Lord of all. Or as Josue puts it: "He is the Lord of all the earth." The pagan who believed is saved. Rahab and her family become members of the Chosen People, while the recently circumcised Israelite is rejected because of his sin.

Here, as often, in the Bible we are confronted with the mystery of the divine choices. We will find them puzzling, perhaps painful, until we learn that only the lowly and the humble win His love.

IT IS THE LORD HIMSELF WHO FIGHTS FOR YOU

In a series of brilliant forays up and down the valleys of Canaan, Josue showed that while his confidence was in the Lord he neglected none of the techniques soldiers like Clausewitz have laid down for the modern military man desirous of victory: mobility, hitting power, protection, morale, Josue used them all. He knew, too, the value of psychological warfare, the power of surprise, the attrition fear can bring, concentration of force at the decisive place and time, the effect of skillful manoeuvre and the inspiration which a quick-witted, intrepid leader alone can give.

But to read the book of Josue as if it were a manual of tactics and strategy would be to miss the true lesson it contains. The sacred writer expresses it clearly for us:

"For not with their own sword did they conquer the land,
    nor did their own arm make them victorious,
But it was Your arm and Your right hand
    and the light of Your countenance, in Your love for them"
(Ps. 43:3f).

God, Josue would have us remember, is faithful to His promises. But these promises are conditional: His help is ours only if we are faithful. He, who is "a holy God, mighty and jealous," did great things for the Israelites and He will do great things for all who serve Him with steadfast love.

These passages show the deep religious values of this book:

"Arise and pass over the Jordan"......................1:1–5:16
"The walls forthwith fell down"......................6:1–27
"Indeed I have sinned against the Lord"..............7:1–8:35

A LEADER OF THE ARMY OF THE LORD

The Josue Roll is one of the treasures of the Vatican Library. It is possibly the most unusual manuscript of the Old Testament in the world. This parchment scroll, thirty-two feet long and twelve inches wide, is covered with illustrations of the book of Josue. The scenes follow one another in uninterrupted succession as in a panorama. Scattered throughout are many little mythological figures personifying the rivers, mountains and cities of Canaan, gaily colored nymphs, sprites and warriors. Important figures are identified as in a modern book of comics. Running captions in cursive Greek help the reader to follow the story, but the graphic line drawings and action figures in blue and violet, brown and red speak for themselves.

To see the Roll for the first time is to be reminded once again that the book of Josue is a military story. Fighting men move quickly across its yellowed surface. The impression given by these vigorous warriors is correct. This book tells a story of conquest and victory won with God's help.

This is the clue to one of the most beautiful — and far too briefly described — incidents in the book. Near Jericho Josue accosted a strange warrior. As Josue advanced the stranger drew his sword. Josue challenged him with the words: "Are you one of ours?" There was no answer. Asked again: "Are you an enemy?", the stranger then spoke: "No, I am a leader of the army of the Lord." We are told that Josue fell to the ground and worshipped him. Was it Michael, "the prince of the heavenly hosts"? Or was it the Lord Himself? We do not know. But we do know that the welcome guest brought the assurance of the divine power which made it possible for the people of God to take possession of Canaan.

ONE IN HEART

From the book of Judges we know that the conquest was not completed during the lifetime of Josue. Yet he accomplished much. At Mount Ebal, he proclaimed the Law of Moses. Deceived by the Gabaonites he made them temple slaves. At Gabaon he routed the enemy and started an argument that is still going on. What really happened when he cried out:

"O sun, do not move at Gabaon;
And O moon, do not move at the valley of Ajalon!"

Was the earth's rotary motion arrested? Is the language figurative or poetical? Did a hailstorm darken the sky? Or was Josue able to accomplish in one day of fighting what normally would have taken him two? We can be sure that the sacred writer is not recording an astronomical observation and we can regret that in the days of Galileo men who were usually prudent tried to offer this text as a lesson in astronomy.

These and other victories enabled Josue to divide the land among the tribes. From Mount Ephraim he continued to act as leader. When he knew that his end was near he summoned the people in order to exhort them to be faithful to God. The unity he desired is the fruit begged for in the Easter postcommunion: "Pour into us, O Lord, the Spirit of Your Love, so that we may by Your loving-kindness be made one in heart."

EASTER WEEK HOMILIES

In the last lenten sermon addressed to the catechumens of the early centuries, they were told that each day during Easter Week they would receive further instruction. Aetheria, the observant pilgrim, who spent a busy spring in Palestine some time during the fourth century, made a note in her travel book of the bishop's exact words:

Lest you who are about to be baptised and to receive the blessed Eucharist should think that anything that is done, is done without meaning, after you have been baptised in the name of God, each day during the octave of Easter all these things will be explained to you in church at the close of Mass.

Some of the paschal homilies have been preserved and it is possible today to re-read the lessons learned so long ago. Much care was taken to show the relation of the New Law to the Old and to link the sacraments of the Church with the corresponding Old Testament figures. In doing this the Fathers were following the example of St. John, who points out in his Gospel that the manna given to the Israelites is a figure of the Eucharist, or of St. Paul, who wrote to the Corinthians that the crossing of the Red Sea is a figure of baptism, or of St. Peter, who explained in his first epistle that the deluge is a figure of the sacrament that has made the catechumens the children of God.

The book of Josue held many lessons for the new Christians. St. Gregory of Nyssa's forthright words were easily understood:

Choose Josue, the son of Nun, for your model. Hold in your hands the book of the Gospel as he carried the Ark. Come out of the desert, that is, leave sin behind. Cross the Jordan. Hasten towards a life lived according to Christ, towards the land which yields fruits of joy and where flow, according to the promise, milk and honey. Overthrow Jericho, that is, your old ways, level its strongholds. All these things have for us an inner meaning because they prefigure realities which are now made clear" (cf. PG 44:420).

In the same spirit St. Cyril of Jerusalem gives several reasons why it was wise for those who love Jesus to make Josue their model:

Josue, the son of Nun, resembles Christ. It was beside the Jordan that he began his leadership of his people; so, too, Christ began His public life after His baptism. The son of Nun selected twelve men to divide the heritage; and Jesus sent into the whole world twelve apostles who were to herald the truth. He, who is a figure, saved Rahab the courtesan because she believed; He, who is the reality, said: 'The publicans and the courtesans will go before you into the kingdom of God.' The walls of Jericho fell at the mere sound of the shouters in the days of the type; at the word of Jesus: 'Not a stone will be left upon a stone,' the Temple of Jerusalem fell before us (cf. PG 33:676).

A LAND FLOWING WITH MILK AND HONEY

Because of his fault Moses, we have seen, could not cross the Jordan and enter Canaan, which had been for so long the object of his desires, but there was another land of promise from which he was not excluded and to which the Church constantly refers during the Easter season. "The Lord hath given you a land flowing with milk and honey," we read in the Easter Monday introit. These words are an invitation to enter His kingdom on earth and to make our own the strength and sweetness that membership in the Church affords, so that some day we will know the greater strength and more perfect sweetness of the true land of promise and the kingdom that has no end.

To that land Jesus, like another Josue crossing the Jordan, will lead us safely past the last barrier which is death. Then He will give us the invitation of the Easter Wednesday introit: "Come, ye blessed of My Father, take possession of the kingdom, alleluia, which has been prepared for you since the foundation of the world." There, at last, in the land where all promises will be fulfilled,

"We shall be emptied and see,
We shall see and know,
We shall know and love
And that in the end without end."

THE BOOK OF JUDGES

THE book of Judges is at times disconcerting. Idolatry, murder, human sacrifice, treachery and revenge are presented with all the harsh realism of a barbarous age. Even the conduct of some of the divinely chosen leaders is singularly unenlightened. What place has such a history in the Bible? What lessons can it teach?

It is a religious history whose heroes must be measured by the stone age standards of their time. It is an episodic history composed of the biographies of twelve charismatic leaders, filled with the Spirit of the Lord, who were raised up at a moment of crisis to deliver a tribe or the whole people from their foes. It is a summary of the adventures of the loosely united descendants of Jacob in the century and a half between the death of Josue and the crowning of King Saul. It is a description of the discouraging situation of a recently nomadic people making spasmodic and uncoordinated efforts to wrest the land from the well-established Canaanites and to resist the attacks of small but aggressive neighbors: the Ammonites strongly entrenched on the other side of the Jordan, the Madianites driven north by drought from the desert, the Moabites guarding the far shores of the Dead Sea, the Philistines, a Cretan people now settled between Israel and the Mediterranean.

Its lesson is one of divine pedagogy. Israel has to learn the costly sequence of infidelity, punishment, repentance, divine intervention and victory. St. Augustine puts the lesson this way: "After the death of Josue, the son of Nun, the people of God had judges, in whose time

62

they were alternately humbled by afflictions on account of their sins, and consoled by prosperity through the compassion of God." This was what usually happened. When the tribes violated the covenant made by Yahweh with Moses on Mount Sinai and adored idols, Yahweh allowed their enemies to chastise them. Difficult days followed until the guilty Israelites acknowledged their faults and pleaded for protection. Then the Spirit of the Lord inspired their leaders and they won welcome, if undeserved, success. That the laws of nature cannot be transgressed with impunity is a lesson a child quickly masters. That God's laws carry an inescapable sanction Israel was slow to remember. So often are we.

BARAC, GEDEON, JEPHTE, SAMSON

This chronicle of a stormy period of Israel's history, like many of the Old Testament books, was not written at one time by a single author. The oral traditions of this heroic age with its mighty exploits and memorable victories were set down in writing at different times, commented on in the Northern and Southern Kingdoms, edited and given a final form centuries after the judges judged Israel.

The term *judge* can be misleading. It is not a synonym for magistrate or ruler. It stands for military and political leaders who liberated their people and became champions of faith in the one, true God. They protected the oppressed and restored the worship of Yahweh. Despite the inertia of many in Israel the judges were able to help men to resist the strong centripetal forces at work in this Hebrew amphictyony which was held together by belief in Yahweh and in the symbol of His presence, the Ark of the Covenant.

Although the theme of the book is soundly theological, few of the Fathers have made special studies of its lessons; when they have done so, their commentaries are usually brief and often allegorical. Nor does the liturgy of the Church unfold for us the book's inner meaning. It is in the epistle to the Hebrews that is stated the divinely inspired message of the judges, "men of whom the world was not worthy." The author declares:

Time will fail me if I tell of Gedeon, of Barac, of Samson, of Jephte, of David, and of Samuel and the prophets, who by *faith*, conquered kingdoms, wrought justice, obtained promises, stopped the mouths of lions, quenched the violence of fire, escaped the edge of the sword, recovered strength from weakness, became valiant in battle, put to flight armies of aliens (11:32–34).

Four of these men of *faith* will be examined in this chapter: Barac, who fought with Debbora; Gedeon, who asked God for a sign; Jephte, who made a rash vow; and Samson, who used and misused his God-given powers. Faith gave victory to these true believers in Yahweh. It is on their faith that we should concentrate not on the crude deeds that belong to an age less cultured than our own.

Those who wish to study all twelve of these divinely-guided leaders may follow this reading plan.

THE POWER OF A WOMAN

Although Josue had brought the Israelites across the Jordan and had worked hard to expel the natives whose civilization was higher than their own, these idolatrous people were still powerful in the plain of Esdraelon after his death. The Canaanite kings hated the Hebrews and they formed a coalition against them. Sisera, their general, controlled the passes of the northern country. Travel was now impossible, caravans had ceased. "Those who traveled the roads went by round about paths. Gone was freedom beyond the walls, gone indeed from Israel" (5:6f).

Debbora, like another Joan of Arc, was chosen by God to free her people. She was renowned for wisdom. Often she was consulted as she sat under her palm tree: men heard her judgments with respect. So when she appealed to Barac, a neighboring Nephtali chieftain, to overcome Sisera, he agreed to do so, but only on these terms: "If you come with me, I will go," he said, "if you do not come with me, I will not go." She promised to accompany him, although she knew that the forces they would lead would be unarmed, for "Not a shield could be seen, nor a lance, among forty thousand in Israel."

Six tribes and some Levites came to fight with Barac. But Debbora had warned him that because of his lack of faith he would gain no glory from the expedition for it was the Lord's will that "Sisera fall into the power of a woman." And so it came to pass.

The motley band of Hebrews took their stand on the slopes of Mount Thabor. Sisera massed his armed men and their chariots in the plain near Megiddo. Yahweh favored the Israelites. When they advanced, the Canaanites faltered, broke ranks and fled. Sisera, escaping by a mountain pass, accepted the hospitality of a woman who offered to hide him in her tent. He did not suspect that her kind words had a treacherous intent so he entered to rest. While he slept, she drove a tent-peg through his head and fastened it to the ground. The enemy had been vanquished, as Debbora had foretold, through the power of a woman.

This grim story is related twice: once in prose, once in poetry. The triumph-song celebrating the victory is one of the finest pieces of ancient Hebrew literature. It is a military ode that expresses the gratitude of a fiercely jubilant people who tenderly loved their warrior God. Cardinal Newman finds that its closing words sum up one of the great lessons of the Old Testament zeal. He says:

What the Old Testament especially teaches us is this: that zeal is as essentially a duty of all God's rational creatures, as prayer and praise, faith and submission; and, surely, if so, especially of sinners whom He has redeemed; that zeal consists in a strict attention to His commands — a scrupulousness, vigilance, heartiness, and punctuality, which bear with no reasoning or questioning about them — an intense thirst for the advancement of His glory — a shrinking from the pollution of sin and sinners — an indignation, nay impatience, at witnessing His honour insulted — a quickness of feeling when His name is mentioned, and a jealousy how it is mentioned — a fulness of purpose, an heroic determination to yield Him service at whatever sacrifice of personal feeling — an energetic resolve to push through all difficulties, were they as mountains, when His eye or hand but gives the sign — a carelessness of obloquy, or reproach, or persecution, a forgetfulness of friend and relative, nay a hatred (so to say) of all that is naturally dear to us, when He says, 'Follow me.' These are some of the characteristics of zeal. Such was the temper of Moses, Phinehas, Samuel, David, Elijah; it is the temper enjoined on all the Israelites, especially on their conduct towards the abandoned nations of Canaan. The text expresses that temper in the words of Debora: 'So let all thine enemies perish, O Lord; but let them that love Him be as the sun when he goeth forth in his might.'

THE LORD IS WITH THEE

The sixth chapter of the book of Judges shows that the Israelites were not long to enjoy peace. Just as they had once invaded Canaan, so now restless nomads from the Arabian desert led by the Madianites made seasonal incursions into Israel. This northward advance of camel-breeding bedouin, who came not to settle but to steal, struck terror into the hearts of the people of God, who had grown lax in their loyalty to Yahweh and were unable to stop the marauders who stripped their fields, robbed their vines, pillaged their towns. Gedeon, "the smiter," was the judge divinely chosen to put an end to this disastrous situation.

The first picture we are given of Gedeon is not promising. Disheartened at rumors of the advance of the Madianites and knowing that they would fill the land like a plague of locusts and waste whatsoever they touched, Gedeon began to thresh and cleanse some wheat so that he and his family might have food for their flight. While he was at work under an oak tree an angel stood at his side and greeted him with the heartening words: "The Lord is with thee, most valiant of men." Gedeon's reply was a direct question: "If the Lord be with us, why have these evils fallen upon us?" And he added: "The Lord brought us out of Egypt. But now the Lord has forsaken us and delivered us into the hands of Madian." The answer he received was a command that carried with it a divine assurance of success: "Go in this thy strength, and thou shalt deliver Israel out of the hand of Madian: know that I have sent thee." Gedeon protested that his family was the least of all in Manasses and that he was the most insignificant member of that family. Then he asked with what means would it be possible for him to deliver Israel. He was given the same response that Moses and Josue had heard before him and that Jeremias, too, in a moment of national peril, would also hear: "I will be with thee." Gedeon did not dare to believe that the Madians would be routed and that this would be accomplished under his leadership. He asked for a sign. Before his wondering eyes the angel touched the rock on which the newly chosen

judge had placed a hastily-assembled sacrifice, and a fire arose from
the rock and consumed the flesh and the unleavened loaves. Then the
angel vanished.

Strong with God-given strength Gedeon began his work. He destroyed an altar of Baal, assembled an intrepid band, defeated the
Madianites, appeased the Ephraimites, exploited his victories, brought
peace to his people, refused the kingship, and gave the glory for all
his exploits to the Lord.

The end of years of oppression, the victory over the enemy, the
ensuing peace and happiness in Israel seemed to the prophet Isaias
worthy to be compared with the triumph and security of God's people
in the messianic age. With prophetic vision he describes the blessings
that would come upon the world when the Prince of Peace would be
born and he gives thanks to God that the yoke wherewith men would
then be laden, the bars that would weigh on their shoulders, the rod that
would long oppress them would be shattered by the Lord even as He
had brought His people peace in the days of Gedeon (Is. 9:26).

The story of this judge ends on an unexpected note but two incidents
of his life can provide material for prayer and will now be examined
in some detail. The first is the "sign" of the fleece; the second is the
stratagem of the lamps.

UNDERSTANDABLE BUT INEXCUSABLE

The Lord had assured Gedeon of victory. The enemy had crossed the
Jordan, messengers had been despatched to muster men in other parts
of Israel. Then Gedeon said to God: "If Thou wilt save Israel by my
hand, as Thou hast said, I will put fleece of wool on the floor. If there
be dew on the fleece only, and if it be dry on all the ground beside, I
shall know that by my hand, as Thou hast said, Thou wilt deliver
Israel."

Not only did the Lord hear this prayer and grant Gedeon the asked-
for "sign" but the next night the request was reversed and the Lord
again complied. What are we to think of the judge's conduct? Is it right
to ask for a sign? Commentators seem to agree that Gedeon's request
for a sign from God of the victory promised to him is understandable
but inexcusable. Saint Thomas is firm about this. There are two ways,
he explains, of asking God for a sign: one, in order "to be instructed
as to what is God's good pleasure in some particular matter," as when
Abraham asked the Lord about the possession of the promised land
(Gen. 15:8), and this is in no way blameworthy; the second, "in order

to test God's power or the truth of His word in some particular matter," as did Gedeon who, "seems to have asked a sign through weakness of faith, wherefore he is not to be excused from sin" (2:2:97:2).

Be all this as it may, the Church has drawn a beautiful lesson from this "sign."

AS DEW UPON THE FLEECE

Explicit references in the Old Testament to Mary are rare. Yet the Fathers, mindful of the preparatory character of the whole Old Testament, have taught us to see a relationship between certain prototypes and the Mother of God. Among the most genuine and the most significant of these symbols is that of Gedeon's fleece. For many centuries it has been a part of Marian iconography and it is beautifully recognized in the liturgy.

The Church, according to the second antiphon of Vespers of the feast of Circumcision, suggests that we see a symbol of Mary's virginal motherhood in the fleece that Gedeon cut from the flesh of his sheep without wounding them, and which when laid on the ground, was found to be all drenched with dew although the ground was dry; and at another time, the fleece remained dry while the ground was damp. This antiphon, repeated so often during the Christmas season in the Little Office of the Blessed Virgin, reads:

"When Thou wast born ineffably of the Virgin, the Scriptures were fulfilled: As dew upon the fleece Thou camest down to save mankind: We praise Thee, O our God."

Saint Bernard comments on these words in his second sermon on the glories of the Virgin Mother. He declares that no one will question that the new canticle which virgins alone shall be allowed to sing in the heavenly kingdom, shall be sung by her who is the Queen of Virgins, and that she shall also sing a second song because she alone of all virgins glories also in being a mother, the Mother of God. Then the saintly abbot of Clairvaux adduces some scriptural testimonies relating to this Virgin Mother and it is in this connection that he alludes to the Psalmist's words on the miracle of the fleece as recorded in the book of Judges. Saint Bernard says:

To this twofold miracle, granted to Gedeon's prayer, the Psalmist seems to refer very beautifully, when he says, speaking of Christ, 'He shall come down like rain upon the fleece, and as showers gently falling upon the earth,' alluding in the first part of the verse to the instance when the fleece was found wet and the floor dry, in the second part to that in which the contrary was the case. For that 'voluntary rain' which

MOSES SHOWING THE TABLES OF THE LAW,
Rembrandt, 1659, Berlin, Kaiser Friedrich Museum, p. 19.

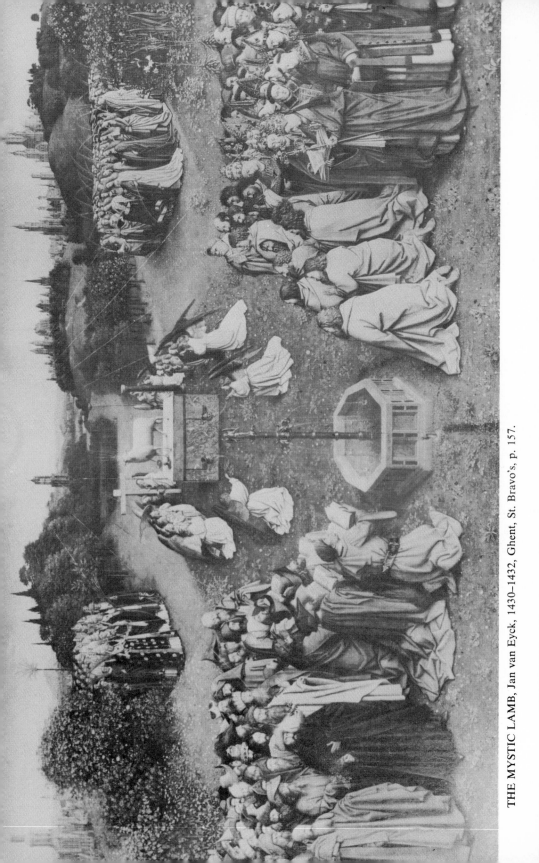

THE MYSTIC LAMB, Jan van Eyck, 1430–1432, Ghent, St. Bravo's, p. 157.

THE GATHERING OF THE MANNA, Dirk Bouts, 1464–1467, Louvain, St. Peter's, p. 21, 36.

EMISSARIES BEFORE JOSHUA, Joshua Roll, Macedonian Manuscript, 7-8th century, Vatican Library, p. 59.

God hath 'set aside for His inheritance' descended first into the Virgin's womb, most gently and softly. . . . Afterwards it was spread through the world . . . amidst the clamour of tongues and the tumult of miracles.

WALKING IN DARKNESS

The second incident from Gedeon's life that we shall discuss here took place during the attack made on the Madian camp. He assembled his three hundred men (the Lord allowed him no larger number lest they glory in their victory and attribute it to their own strength). He told each one to take a trumpet and an empty pitcher and to place a lighted lamp within each pitcher. At midnight he and his men surrounded the dark and silent camp. At his order they sounded their trumpets, broke their pitchers and easily defeated their confused and howling foe.

This is one of the passages that John of the Cross uses to illustrate his chapter in *The Ascent of Mount Carmel* entitled: "How faith is the proximate and proportionate means to the understanding whereby the soul may attain to the divine union of love." Darkness, the Saint explains, often is used in sacred Scripture to signify the obscurity of faith wherein the Divinity is hidden when it communicates itself to the soul and which will be ended when, as St. Paul says, that which is in part shall be ended (this is the darkness of faith) and that which is perfect shall come (this is the divine light). The Carmelite reformer continues:

Of this we have a good illustration in the army of Gedeon, whereof it is said that all the soldiers had lamps in their hands, which they saw not because they had them concealed in the dark pitchers; and when these pitchers were broken, the light was seen. Just so does faith, which is foreshadowed by these pitchers, contain within itself the divine light; which when it is ended and broken, at the ending and breaking of this mortal life, will allow the glory and light of the Divinity, which was contained in it to appear.

The Saint concludes that if the soul in this world is to attain to union with God, it must enter into this darkness of faith, holding in its hands (that is in the works of its will) the light which is the union of love, so that when "the pitchers of this life are broken by death the soul may see God face to face in glory."

INTRINSICALLY WRONG

Jephte is the third judge who is praised by the author of Hebrews. The story opens on a familiar note: "The children of Israel, adding new sins to their old ones, did evil in the sight of the Lord, and served idols." Jephte seemed the man least likely to save them. Rejected by his half-brothers and refused any share in the family patrimony, he had left Galaad and won a reputation for valor as an outlaw. The Israelites sent a delegation to ask him to be their leader and to defend them against the Ammonites, a Trans-jordanic people related to the Moabites (for both were said to have been descended from Lot). The exiled bandit knew these troublesome neighbors and he agreed to return and help the Israelites on condition that he be recognized as their permanent ruler in the event of victory.

The battle was fought and won. But this success is not what men remember today when they recall his name; instead they speak of a vow he made and unwisely kept. Before engaging with the Ammonites this was what he had vowed to the Lord: "If Thou wilt deliver the children of Ammon into my hands, whosoever shall first come out of the doors of my house, and shall meet me when I return in peace from the children of Ammon, the same will I offer as a holocaust to the Lord." The Lord gave him victory and, although his vow was intrinsically wrong and therefore invalid, he sacrificed his only child, a loved little daughter who led the band of young girls who came with timbrel and dance to welcome the conquering hero home.

Such sacrifices were not unknown in antiquity. It is related that Alexander the Great made a similar vow to sacrifice whatever first met his eye. Meeting a man riding an ass, he started to throttle the man, then realizing that he had first seen the ass, he destroyed the animal instead. Less fortunate than Alexander, Idomeneus, legendary Cretan king, was caught in a storm, sailing home from the Trojan War. He vowed to sacrifice to Poseidon, if he reached port safely, the first living thing that he met after landing. As the boat neared land his only son hurried to be the first to embrace him. Idomeneus kept his promise but the sacrifice of the boy released a whole series of disasters and the king was driven from Crete. Yet we cannot conclude from this that such an act was unpleasing in the eyes of the ancients because Agamemnon, sacrificing his daughter Iphigenia, was praised because he won for himself favorable winds on his way to Troy.

Human sacrifice was not unknown in Israel but it was held in abhorrence and the sacred writer who relates the rash vow does so quite objectively and without comment. What comments have authors made since then? St. Thomas says that Jephte's vow should not have been kept and he quotes with approval the words of St. Jerome: "In vowing he was foolish, through lack of discretion, and in keeping the vow he was wicked." Then he adds with unexpected clemency:

Yet it is premised that 'the Spirit of the Lord came upon him' because his faith and his devotion which moved him to make that vow, were from the Holy Ghost; and for this reason he is reckoned among the saints, as also by reason of the victory he obtained, and because it is probable that he repented of his sinful deed, which nevertheless foreshadowed something good (2:2:88:2).

Dante's comment is constructive. He advises: "Be loyal and not squint-eyed, as was Jephte in his firstling vow; whom it more became to say: 'I did amiss,' than keep it and do worse."

Cornelius a Lapide is understanding and generous in his judgment. He admits that the vow was illicit and impious yet finds a number of plausible reasons why he believes that Jephte can be excused in whole or in part:

1. He acted through ignorance and zeal.
2. He thought he was bound by his vow.
3. He lived in a rude age, lacking in subtle distinctions.
4. He was a military man trained to keep his word.
5. He had no prophet or high priest to whom he could submit his case of conscience.
6. He is praised in the New Testament and included among the list of heroes by the author of Ecclesiasticus, so why should we condemn him?

Finally, to extenuate but not to condone his deed, it should be remembered that the Hebrews believed that a vow once pronounced, like a blessing, could not be revoked because it had an independent existence of its own. Moses had warned the Israelites of this with these words: "If a man make a vow to the Lord . . . he shall fulfill all that he has promised" (Num. 3:30). Jephte's daughter seems to have been aware of this and concluded that her father should keep his vow because God had crowned it with victory. She assured him: "My father, if thou hast opened thy mouth to the Lord, do unto me whatsoever thou hast promised, since victory hath been granted to thee, and revenge of thy enemies."

SELF-KILLED, NOT WILLINGLY

Faith was the quality in Samson that was praised by the author of the epistle to the Hebrews yet it was for his strength that he is largely remembered today. The story was a favorite of Baroque artists in the seventeenth century because of its drama and heroism. The blood-shed of the Thirty Years' War gave men a taste for the startling and the horrible. These notes mark the four masterpieces Rembrandt painted during that sanguinary religious war and which illustrate important moments in the Samson story.

The first is entitled "The Sacrifice of Manoah" and shows a nameless guest vanishing in the flames of a sacrifice that a pious couple of Dan offered in gratitude when they were told that their child would be blessed by God, to whom the boy must be specially dedicated. "Samson's wedding feast" is the second picture Rembrandt painted of this strong and resourceful man who so unwisely chose a wife among the hated Philistines. The third picture, "Samson threatening his father-in-law," shows the giant who had vanquished the Philistines, berating the father of his bride who had decided that he would not recognize the Herculean hero as his son-in-law. Cunning, cruel Samson was a true believer in Yahweh, to whom he owed his strength in virtue of his dedication, but his conduct was guided by no strict moral code and he easily fell a victim to the wiles of a scheming woman, Dalila. To her he revealed the secret of his strength : "No razor has touched my head, for I have been consecrated to God from my mother's womb. If I am shaved, my strength will leave me, and I shall be as weak as any other man." The traitoress had only to cut his hair and call the Philistines, who blinded the now-powerless Hebrew hero. Rembrandt in the last picture portrays what happened next. The Philistines gouged out his eyes. Samson now lies weakly on the ground and Dalila escapes, blood dripping from her hands. It is realistic and ugly.

In the medieval period artists were not interested in the gruesome scenes that were to be popular in the seventeenth century but they preferred to paint the last incident of Samson's life, in which they recognized him to be a figure of Christ who by dying destroyed the forces of evil. Samson was now the plaything of the Philistines, who took him from prison only to mock him at their banquets. In the long, dark hours of solitude Samson acknowledged his errors and implored the Lord's forgiveness. One day when his tormentors brought him to amuse a great gathering, he seized the pillars of the huge hall. During his imprisonment his hair had grown and his strength had returned, so with the words: "Strengthen me, O God . . . Let me die with the Philistines," he pushed hard, the building fell — he and all the people perished.

The tragic magnificence of his last moments have been wonderfully captured by Milton in *Samson Agonistes*. Like St. Augustine, Milton felt obligated to clear the hero of the guilt of suicide. Milton does so in these words: "Samson," he says,

"Thou now ly'st victorious
Among thy slain *self-killed*
Not willingly, but tangled in the fold
Of dire necessity, whose law in death conjoined
Thee with thy slaughtered foe."

St. Augustine explains it in these words: "Samson, who drew down the house upon himself and his foes together, is justified only on this ground, that the Spirit who wrought wonders by him had given him strict instructions to do this." While a modern moral theologian suggests that he might be exonerated on the grounds that he willed his own death only indirectly as a means of destroying the Philistines and that in the last analysis he acted for the common good. Finally, we must remember that the graces given these charismatic leaders were given for the sake of others and did not necessarily sanctify the recipients; they brought liberation for the Israelites but were not always wisely used by the judges to whom they were entrusted.

INDEPENDENCE . . . ACTIVISM . . . DISCOURAGEMENT

The liturgy, as we have said, rarely quotes from the book of Judges, yet this does not mean that the struggles of Debbora, Gedeon, Jephte and Samson do not help us to understand the official prayer of the Church. In fact, we find in the liturgy and in the book of Judges, as a recurring *motif*, the same martial note. Life is a warfare. In the *Sanctus* of the Mass, each day we hail the "Holy, holy, holy, Lord God of armies." In moments of great triumph we sing: "Christ conquers! Christ rules! Christ reigns!"

The battle that was joined in the garden of Genesis will go on until the end of time. If we are to emerge victorious we must enlist the help of our warrior God, we must avoid the independence, the activism, the discouragement into which the Israelites so often fell.

They loved to act independently of God. Like worldlings of every age they sometimes failed to see the beauty of obedience and submission to the Law because this requires a depth of insight the superficial never reach and supposes a willingness to serve that the proud never understand. Self-seeking, self-assertion, self-aggrandizement yield bitter fruits of frustration and failure. Only to the dependent, the submissive and the obedient does God grant victory.

There was in their efforts a consistent, though usually implicit, affirmation of what might be called activism, a belief that they could conquer their foes by their own strength. We, too, are often blind to the primacy of the supernatural. In the important initiatives of zeal only the truly interior soul realizes the full value of divine means: prayer, charity, humility, docility to grace, close union with God. Once these are assured, then human means can be safe and effective: until these divine means have been achieved it is perilous to proceed.

A third error is discouragement. For us who have meditated on Christ crucified, the divine paradox of success through failure ought to be a mystery full of light and courage. What we see in our lives as checks and obstacles are the means God has chosen to perfect His instruments and complete His plan. He cannot fail, nor can we when we place all our trust in Him. Progress, results, measurement of growth are words that come cynically to our lips when we are discouraged and are tempted to judge by human standards. 'The uselessness of it all' is a whining complaint that faith never fostered. 'I cannot go on' is a cowardly surrender that hope never inspired. 'This is asking too much' is a miserly admission that we do not know the meaning of love.

The road may wind up-hill all the way but whether we are just setting out or are well on our journey or in sight of the summit, we must be realists. We must see the reality that God is all and we are nothing. Then there will be no faint-heartedness, no trust in merely human measures, no foolish counting on our own strength.

This ought to be easy for us because we have the example of the judges to hearten us. Or, to quote the words of the author of the epistle to the Hebrews:

Therefore let us also, having such a cloud of witnesses over us, put away every encumbrance and the sin entangling us, and run with patience to the fight set before us; looking towards the author and finisher of faith, Jesus, who for the joy set before Him, endured a cross, despising shame, and sits at the right hand of the throne of God. Consider, then, Him who endured such opposition from sinners against Himself, so that you may not grow weary and lose heart. (12:1–3)

THE BOOK OF RUTH

IT WAS springtime in the land of Moab. There men learned that the famine in Juda had come to an end. So Noemi prepared to return to the country of her fathers.

The ten years spent on the fertile plateau southeast of the Dead Sea had been marked by sorrow. First her husband had died, then her two sons. She was poor. Some property in Bethlehem was hers if she would claim it, and so she explained her plan to Orpha and to Ruth, her devoted Moabite daughters-in-law. Kissing them she said: "Go back, each of you to your mother's house! May the Lord be kind to you as you were to the departed and to me! May the Lord grant each of you husbands and a home in which you will find rest."

The two young women declared that they would not leave her. Noemi insisted. Sorrowing, Orpha obeyed. "See now," the older woman said to the weeping Ruth, "your sister-in-law has gone back to her people and to her god." Firmly came the answer: "Do not ask me to abandon or forsake you! For wherever you go, I will go, wherever you lodge I will lodge, your people shall be my people, your God my God."

The bond of tender affection uniting Ruth to Noemi was all the stronger because of the second bond of her love for the true God. Loyalty to her mother-in-law meant also fidelity to Yahweh. Noemi could make no further objection. Together the two women set out.

MAY YOU RECEIVE A FULL REWARD

When they climbed the rugged hills of Juda that day in April long ago when the Judges judged Israel, they found the barley fields ready for the harvest. All Bethlehem was astir. There was sympathy for Noemi, admiration that deepened to respect for Ruth when men learned her story and watched her as she resolutely set to work to support her mother-in-law and herself.

Noemi was mindful of the injunction given by Moses: "When you reap the harvest in your field and overlook a sheaf there, you shall not go back to get it; let it be for the alien, the orphan or the widow, that the Lord your God may bless you in all your undertakings" (Deut. 24:19). So she bade Ruth go to the barley fields and glean after the reapers.

The owner, coming to the field where Ruth was working, learned the name of the beautiful stranger and how she had worked all day with scarcely a moment's rest. To Ruth he said: "Listen, my daughter! Do not go to glean in anyone else's field; you are not to leave here. Stay with my women servants. . . . When you are thirsty, you may go and drink from the vessels the young men have filled."

He added that he had heard of her courage in leaving Moab and he begged Yahweh to bless her: "May the Lord reward what you have done! May you receive a full reward from the Lord, the God of Israel, under whose wings you have come for refuge." Then bidding her share his lunch, he secretly told his servants to drop handfuls of grain and to allow her to glean among the sheaves so as to lighten her work.

BOOZ . . . OBED . . . JESSE . . . DAVID

That evening Ruth told all to Noemi, offering as proof of the owner's generosity a large quantity of barley and some of the roasted grain that she had saved from lunch. With Noemi's blessing, Ruth returned to the same fields each day until the barley and the wheat had all been harvested.

Seven weeks passed, and Noemi now spoke to Ruth. She explained that the owner of the field was Booz, her dead husband's kinsman. And she told Ruth to go to the threshing floor and there, unobserved by curious eyes, to ask Booz to be her protector, her *goel*. This interesting word occurs, in various forms, 22 times in this book. An appeal is made to a *goel* when life, liberty or possessions are in jeopardy.

Here Ruth's appeal to Booz refers only to land. Noemi hoped that he would intervene and save the land that was rightfully hers. She may also have hoped that after protecting the family possessions he would make the young widow his wife. According to the Law of Moses when a man died childless, his brother (in Hebrew, *levir*) or his next-of-kin had to marry the widow. A levirate marriage ensured the continuation of the family name. The book of Deuteronomy prescribes that: "The first-born son she bears shall continue the line of the deceased brother, that his name may not be blotted out from Israel" (25:5–10).

Dutifully Ruth obeyed. Symbolically covering her with his robe, Booz blessed Yahweh because of her fidelity to the customs of her adopted people and he promised to arrange all as she wished.

The hallowed ending of the stories first heard in childhood, "and they lived happily ever after," would seem a fitting close to the four delightful chapters that compose the book of Ruth and which should be read in their entirety. The beauty of their form and content has made them one of the treasures of world literature. One that is all the more unusual in that it portrays a mother-in-law who deserves to be the patroness of that much-maligned group. She was noble, unselfish, deeply religious and very kind. Deservedly she shared in the new couple's happiness. Hers was one day to be the joy of holding in her arms the son of Ruth and Booz. The baby was called Obed. He was the father of Jesse and the grandfather of David.

So it came about that Ruth the Moabite, the stranger who left her people and her country, was loved by Yahweh and was privileged to become one of the ancestors of His Incarnate Son. St. Matthew includes her name in the genealogy of Jesus. "Booz begot Obed of Ruth, Obed begot Jesse, Jesse begot David the king" (1:5). This is a reminder each time we read the first chapter of the first Gospel that all men of every race are dear in God's sight.

Spiritual writers suggest that Ruth prefigures our Lady, through whose divine maternity all peoples form part of the Mystical Body of her divine Son.

BECAUSE OF CHRIST THE LORD

Ruth's place in the genealogy of our Lord impressed the fifth century Theodoret of Cyrus, one of the few Fathers to write about this book. He prefaces his brief commentary with the question: "Why is the story of Ruth recorded?" His answer is concise: "First of all, because of Christ the Lord. He is descended from her according to the flesh." Theodoret then tells how the Moabite was chosen in preference to Sara, Rebecca and other holy women, and he lists the examples of virtue that the book contains.

Josephus, the first century Jewish historian, sees in the genealogy a reason for him to include her story in his compilation known as *Jewish*

Antiquities. He concludes his summary of the book with these words: "This story of Ruth I have been constrained to relate, being desirous to show the power of God and how easy it is for Him to promote even ordinary folk to rank so glorious as that to which He raised David, sprung from such ancestors."

THE HEART OF YOUR HANDMAID

Much of the charm of the book of Ruth comes from the dignity and beauty of the family as it is pictured for us in ancient Israel. The book of Judges gives a cruder impression of these days, and it is good to know that there was another and a more pleasant side to life in Palestine before the days of King David. The language and style of the book suggest an author living in the days of that beloved monarch, but the rites and customs belong to a much earlier age.

Each year at Pentecost this book is always read by the Jews. It has no equivalent place in the Latin breviary. But we have seen that Ruth's name is honored whenever the opening chapter of St. Matthew's Gospel is read. Noemi's answer to the women of Bethlehem who came to welcome her after her long stay in Moab are adapted in the first responsory of the feast of the Seven Sorrows of our Lady: "Call me not Noemi (that is beautiful), but call me Mara (that is bitter), for the Almighty has filled me with bitterness" (1:20). And Ruth's reply to Booz when he praised her devotedness to her mother-in-law is found in the third responsory of the feast of Mary's Immaculate Heart: "I have found grace in Your eyes, my Lord; You have comforted me and spoken to the heart of Your handmaid" (2:13). More important is the allusion to this book that is found in the prayers of the Mass.

THE LORD BE WITH YOU

Eight times during holy Mass the priest repeats a phrase from the book of Ruth. The greeting given by Booz to his reapers, "The Lord be with you," introduces the prayer of the four main parts of the Mass: at the reading service, at the offertory, at the Canon, and at the Communion. At a solemn Mass the deacon makes this proclamation before reading the Gospel and before the dismissal. It also is said at the foot of the altar and before the last Gospel.

This liturgical greeting is found in several places in the Bible. Besides its use in the book of Ruth, we find it in the book of Judges. When the angel of Yahweh appeared to Gedeon, he said: "The Lord is with you, O most valiant of men" (6:12f.). The prophet Azarias drew the special lesson that man's happiness is measured by his fidelity to God when he admonished Asa, king of Juda, with the words: "The Lord is with you when you are with Him" (2 Par. 15:2). When the archangel appeared to our Lady, he said: "Hail, full of grace, the Lord is with you" (Luke 1:28).

These words in the Mass are always an invitation to pinpoint our attention on what is about to take place. They are a reminder that the Mass is the offering of priest and people. Father Jungmann suggests that we express their meaning in some such words as these: "Brethren in Christ, we are going to pray. Devout Christians, listen to today's Gospel." This call to closer participation enables the people to return the greeting and strengthens their awareness of God's presence.

The response the people make also has a Hebrew origin. St. Paul offers many parallels (e.g., 2 Tim. 4:22). The reply of the reapers to Booz was: "May the Lord bless you." Our formula, "And with your spirit," has the same meaning. The Semitism "your spirit" means "you." It is really the response: "May the Lord also be with you."

St. John Chrysostom in his first Pentecost sermon suggests that we look for a still deeper meaning. He sees in the words "your spirit" a reference to the indwelling Holy Spirit, and a reminder that the prelate offers the Sacrifice in the power of the Third Person of the Blessed Trinity. In the ordination of deacons and priests the Holy Spirit is solemnly called down upon those who are about to be ordained, so it is the deacon and the priest alone who have the right to give this greeting and to hear the people's respectful acknowledgment of the presence of the "Spirit" whom His sacred ministers have received in so special a manner.

THE PRAISE OF HESED

The Hebrew word *hesed* challenges translators. Lexicons list many synonyms, yet none of them succeed in capturing all the modalities of goodness, divine and human, that the word contains. To consider it in the book of Ruth is to see its many meanings concretized and *hesed* becomes a warm, living, lovely thing. The theme of this book is *the praise of hesed*. This is the praise of God's mercy for man, the praise of man's loving service of God, the praise of man's pity for other men.

When God so blessed a Moabite, the *hesed*, the loving-kindness He showed to a woman of a neighboring enemy tribe, prefigured the love He would one day pour out on all men, and prepared them to welcome Gentile as well as Jew into His kingdom. When Noemi bade farewell to Orpha and Ruth, she blessed the affectionate young widows, and she asked Yahweh to show them His *hesed*, His divine mercy which fills the soul with peace and a security nothing human can destroy. When Booz made Ruth welcome and asked her to glean in no other field, he showed *hesed*, a gentle pity for one in need. When Ruth asked Booz to be her *goel*, he praised her *hesed*, her loyal obedience to Yahweh's laws, her unselfish service of Noemi.

AMID THE ALIEN CORN

These attractive qualities have made the book of Ruth a favorite among artists. Murillo painted a large picture of Ruth and Noemi leaving Moab while Orpha turns back to her family's home. In the Louvre are two paintings in which we see Ruth gleaning in the fields. The first was made for Cardinal Richelieu by Poussin. Women are busily at work in the large field. In the foreground Ruth kneels before Booz in a gesture of gratitude for his generosity. In the second picture Van Dyck shows the young gleaner amid the ripened grain. Here is all the swiftness, clarity and glowing vitality that we associate with this careful artist.

Poets, too, praise Ruth. Hood thinks of her joy when she stood in the fields "Clasp'd by the golden light of the morn." Keats' concept is more somber. In his *Ode to the Nightingale*, he writes:

> The voice I heard this passing night was heard
> In ancient days by emperor and clown:
> Perhaps the self-same song that found a path
> Through the sad heart of Ruth, when sick for home,
> She stood in tears amid the alien corn.

GLEAN IN NO OTHER FIELD

Monsignor Ronald Knox has written a movingly beautiful little book on the Blessed Sacrament. It is entitled *The Window in the Wall*. One of the sermons it contains is based on a sentence taken from the book of Ruth. It is Noemi's question to Ruth after her first day spent in the barley fields: "Where did you glean today?" And the Monsignor, remembering a chapter in an old-fashioned book of meditations entitled *The Field of the Holy Eucharist*, shows that "The harvest which was sown in tears on Maundy Thursday is reaped with joy on Corpus Christi." Christ's own Body illustrates the law that is operative in the lives of each of His followers: "Unless the grain of wheat falling into the ground die, itself remains alone. But if it die, it brings forth much fruit" (John 12:24).

It is ours now to reap a harvest from our visits to the Blessed Sacrament and our reception of holy Communion. That is what the saints did, and will we be content, like Ruth, merely to glean while the reapers carry away rich sheaves?

Discouraged we may be with our own poor gleaning. Dryness may so dishearten us that, famished for what appeals to the senses, we may want to leave Bethlehem (which means in Hebrew "house of bread") and go into the green fields of Moab. But like Noemi and Ruth let us return to that high city of Juda where the Master of the Harvest will repeat to us the words of Booz to Ruth: "Glean in no other field," for in "the Field of the Holy Eucharist" is hidden the great treasure, which will be ours if we are willing to give Him all He asks.

THE BOOKS OF SAMUEL

DURING THE forty
days between Easter and the Ascension, St. Luke tells us that Jesus
spoke to the disciples about the kingdom of God (Acts 1:3). At a
crucial moment of His public ministry He had said that His privileged
followers would some day know the mysteries of this kingdom — and
the Church has made it her primary concern to unfold these mysteries
to the faithful during the first six weeks of "the long afternoon of the
liturgical year," the period between Pentecost and Advent.

KINGDOM OF ISRAEL

In the breviary lessons of the first six weeks after Pentecost the kingdom of God is presented in a series of incidents taken from the Old
Testament. All of these stories of the kingdom in Israel are in a sense
prophetic. Each tells us something about the kingdom of Christ that
the future would reveal.

Looking back three thousand years we can see, in the story of the
establishment of the kingdom in Israel and in the history of the first
two kings, types of the Church that Christ came on earth to found. The
Ascension did not put an end to His mission. It is completed by the
Holy Spirit under whose guidance the words of Sacred Scripture still
bring life and light to men.

BOOKS OF SAMUEL AND BOOKS OF KINGS

The lessons of the first nocturn are from books of Samuel. They
cover a little more than a century — the years between the establish-

ment of the Israelite monarchy and the death of David. Three men dominate this turning point in the history of the people of God: the saintly Samuel, and the two kings whom he anointed at the Lord's command: Saul, "the man after the people's heart," and David, "the man after God's heart."

According to an old Jewish tradition the two books of Samuel were originally a single volume. The Greeks who translated the Hebrew Bible into their language treated them as a unit, but for practical purposes they divided them into two nearly equal parts and combined them with two books of Kings which contained further details of the kingdom until its destruction in 586 B.C. St. Jerome preserved this arrangement when he translated the books into Latin and called them the four books of Kings. So the two books of Samuel are found in some Catholic Bibles as the first two books of Kings.

The Hebrew tradition, which named these books "the books of *Samuel*" did not mean to attribute their authorship to him. Like the titles *Josue* or *Job*, a leading character is indicated. Modern scholars believe that some unknown author in the eighth century B.C. combined several documents so as to present the biographies of Samuel, Saul and David in a single dramatic narrative.

The sources he chose were valuable, but he failed to eliminate all repetitions and he neglected to explain some obscure points. The "royal annals of the court of David" that he inserted in 2 Samuel 9–20 are one of the finest examples of historical writing that can be found in the ancient world. Poetry of exceptional beauty is also included with the prose documents. When Samuel's mother learned that God had heard her prayer and that she would have a son she sang a canticle of joy (1 Sam. 2:1–10). It is interesting to compare Anna's words with the song that the sister of Moses composed on an occasion of great national rejoicing (Deut. 32) and with Our Lady's *Magnificat* (Luke 1:46–55), which is recited every day at Vespers. Another beautiful poem is found in 2 Sam. 22:1–31. This is David's exultant hymn of thanksgiving which is repeated in Psalm 17 and forms part of the divine office for Monday Matins.

Other passages that are well worth reading are listed here:

First Book of Samuel
"May the Lord grant thy prayer"......................1:1–28
"Speak, Lord, Thy servant is listening"................3:1–21
"Five golden mice".................................6:1–21

PURPOSE

What unifying purpose guided the anonymous author of the books of Samuel? He wished to show that the kingdom of the people of God was a divine institution and that God's loving care, so evident in the first years of the monarchy, would be extended to the Davidic dynasty forever. In the light of fulfilment we can see that the perpetuity of this kingdom is to be found in the kingdom established by Christ.

HISTORICAL BACKGROUND

To understand the lessons from the books of Samuel that are proposed for our contemplation by the Church it is helpful to know their historical frame of reference.

After the death of Moses, who led the Israelites out of Egypt into the Promised Land, Josue conquered Canaan. The next two centuries are known as "the days when the judges judged Israel." These local military heroes and men of God guided the destinies of the autonomous tribes who had conquered the land of the Canaanites which had been assigned to them by lot. Occasionally two or three tribes formed a temporary alliance. But in peaceful times each tribe acted as an independent unit despite the common bonds of race and religion. "In those days there was no king in Israel and every man did what was right in his own eyes" (Jdgs. 17:6).

Challenged by a new danger the Israelites asked for a king. The great threat to their independent tribal existence came from the Philistines, a "sea-people" who had recently left their homeland in the Aegean. They had settled on the coastal strip between the territory of the Israelites and the Mediterranean. Needing more land they advanced eastward. This brought them to the territory occupied by the twelve tribes. This land they were never to conquer, but centuries later the Romans were to give the whole region a latinized form of their name, *Palestina*.

The Philistines were an energetic, ambitious people. They were well governed. They were skillful military strategists. They enjoyed a monopoly of a new metal that made them far superior to the Israelites, who had no iron for their swords or chariots or plows.

Realists among the twelve tribes feared that the dynamic invaders would soon be their rulers and they demanded that the men of Israel submit to a central authority. This was the appeal they brought to Samuel: "Make us a king to judge us and fight our battles for us and we will be like all the other nations."

Samuel represented in his own person all the offices Israel had hitherto recognized: he was a Nazarite (Sam. 1:11), he was a judge (7:15–17), he was a Levite (3:1) and a prophet or a seer (9:9). He listened to the people's petition. He reminded them that God had long been their leader and that an earthly king would oppress the people who had chosen him. They rejected his warning. Saul became their first king.

Chosen by God, anointed by Samuel, acclaimed by the people, Saul began his reign with every assurance of success. The war of liberation against the Philistines drove the invaders toward the coast. But a disastrous defeat at Gelboe was the occasion of Saul's death and the Philistines marched towards the Jordan, cutting off the northern from the southern tribes. David, the friend of whom Saul had been madly jealous, was anointed king by Samuel. At first only the men of Juda acknowledged his sovereignty (2 Sam. 2).

David was a man of courage and political vision. Strong in the knowledge that God had chosen him to lead his people, he freed himself from tribal rivalries. He chose Jerusalem for his capital. This was his by right of conquest. Here he brought the ark and made the city on Mount Moriah a holy city, the center of the political and religious life of a united Israel.

His victories over the often-victorious Philistines transformed these once powerful adversaries into vassals who were no longer able to maintain the iron monopoly that had ensured their supremacy. He reduced to submission his neighbors beyond the Jordan and those south of the Dead Sea. Peace brought him control of the trade routes between Arabia and Syria.

These military achievements almost eclipse his administrative suc-

cess. No detail of civil or military or religious life was neglected. The
country was wisely governed and prosperous. David was a well-loved
king, but he knew many sorrows and he died a saddened, lonely old
man.

RELIGIOUS MESSAGE

Yet it was not to review the rising and falling fortunes of the ancient
eastern Mediterranean world that the two books of Samuel were placed
among the inspired writings of the Bible, or were selected for the divine
office. They are part of the Church's official prayer because they contain a religious message: they show us the conditions and the problems of God's kingdom on earth.

Although the form of government had changed since the days of the
patriarchs, the twelve tribes were God's Chosen People and the new
king was God's deputy and must rule in His name. The Hebrew king
is called "the son of God" (2 Sam. 7:14) and when, like Saul, he
fails to rule with God's spirit then he is rejected (1 Sam. 15:35).
The profoundly theocratic nature of the kingdom affected the lives
of all the citizens. David revived the religious fervor of his people: the
transfer of the ark of the covenant to Jerusalem (2 Sam. 6:1–23), the
organization of the divine worship (1 Par. 23:1–26:32), his preparations for the building of a glorious temple (1 Par. 17:1–27), his legacy
to the people of a great collection of psalms (e.g. Psalms 1–40 are
attributed to him).

But the most important spiritual values of the books of Samuel are
to be found in their relation to the messianic kingdom of Christ.

David's work was soon undone. Solomon, his son and successor, was
the last king of a united Israel. The divided nation was eventually
swept away in the clashing power politics of contenders for world
supremacy in the Near East. But David's greater achievement survived: he had founded a kingdom with a deeply religious purpose. This
was the preparation for a kingdom that would never pass. The people
of Israel, freed from their enemies, represented the Christian people
freed from spiritual foes. The Davidic dynasty prefigured the eternal
kingship of Christ who was born in the city of David and of whose
kingdom there will be no end.

A final question remains to be considered: in proposing for our
prayer the three great figures of Samuel, Saul and David, what lessons
does the Church wish us to learn? Each of these leaders well repays
special study.

SAMUEL

Samuel is another John the Baptist. He was God's answer to the prayer of a mother long without a child (1 Sam. 1–2). From his earliest days he was dedicated to the service of God and had made his own the perfect prayer: "Speak, Lord, for thy servant heareth" (1 Sam. 3:1–21). He fearlessly defended God's rights (1 Sam. 13:15). He prepared the way for the king and stepped aside when his work was done (1 Sam. 9:1–10:27).

SAUL

So Samuel, the selfless servant of God, was succeeded by Saul. If Samuel is given to us as a model, Saul is given as a warning. He is the soul that fails. Why did he fail? Why was he rejected by God?

There are many facets to the answer. Saul was distinguished for courage, modesty of manner, military skill. His first forays against the Philistines were victorious. In spite of his success or perhaps because of it he turned away from God. He was guided by what St. Paul calls "the wisdom of this world." Twice he was found wanting.

The first fault was committed at Galgal. Fearing that the people would desert him if he waited until Samuel came, he offered sacrifice. This was a sacrilege that had been severely punished in the past: Core was swallowed up in the earth for a similar crime. Only a priest or a prophet had this right. So Samuel condemned the guilty king: "Thy kingdom shall not continue. The Lord hath sought him a man according to his own heart: and him hath the Lord commanded to be prince over His people, because thou hast not observed that which the Lord commanded" (1 Sam. 13:1–14).

Saul's second fault was one of disobedience. He was told to destroy the Amalecites. But he spared the king and his rich flocks because "he feared the people and he obeyed their voice" (1 Sam. 15:1–35). God rejected Saul because Saul rejected God.

Here was a man who lacked "fear of the Lord." According to Newman: "Unbelief and wilfullness are the wretched characteristics of Saul's history."

These led to the moods of melancholy and jealousy that darkened his last days. A visitor to the *Mauritshuis* in the Hague is long haunted by the bitterness and the despair on the face of the king whom Rembrandt painted in all the regal splendor of the east. The ruler is seated opposite David, the young harpist, who is wholly absorbed in his playing. The folds of a soft dark curtain separating the figures

suggest Saul's loneliness of soul. Two gestures reveal the conflicting
tendencies that strove for mastery in the man who was never able to
understand that "sanctity is generosity, consistent and unremitting."
With one hand he tries to wipe away a tear, for David's music had
touched his heart. But his face is hard and his features betray a relent-
less inner fury, as does his other hand which reaches for his jeweled
javelin. David could tell him of the peace which humility can give but,
as Browning puts it, Saul would fail, because he could never understand
the harpist's words:

> I, David, ever renew
> (With that stoop of the soul which in bending upraises it too)
> The submission of man's nothing-perfect to God's all-complete,
> As by each new obeisance in spirit I climb to His feet.

DAVID

David, too, had his faults, but each failure brought him back to God,
and therefore men of every age acknowledge his greatness.

When Dante reached the sixth heaven, the abode of the just kings,
the blessed spirits in that realm of radiant light welcomed him with
the opening words of the book of Wisdom: "Love justice, you who
are judges of the earth." Here Dante found David, the greatest king of
Israel. Unlike the rejected Saul whom he succeeded, David is a man
of justice, the beloved of God, faithful and obedient.

The Fathers of the Church speak eloquently of the many ways his
life resembles the life of Jesus: in his birth in the same city, in his
persecution by those he loved, in his glory. Abandoned by his followers
David had to flee from Jerusalem: our Lord deserted by His disciples
went from that city to His death.

David served God faithfully and God rewarded him with divine
liberality. Nathan's prophecy addressed to the king crowned the many
promises given through the centuries to a sinful world. Men knew that
the Redeemer would belong to the race of the woman (Gen. 3:15),
to the descendants of Sem (Gen. 9:26), to the children of Abraham
(Gen. 12:2) and to the tribe of Juda (Gen. 49:10). Now it was
revealed that He would come from the house and the family of David
(1 Par. 17:10–14).

During the darkest days of the history of the Chosen People, their
prophets reminded them of this great promise (Amos 9:11 ; Osee 3:5 ;
Is. 9:1–6). When the enemy was about to destroy Jerusalem, Jeremias
affirmed that the dynasty of David would be re-established (Jer. 30:9).

During the exile, Ezechiel declared that another David would one day lead the people of God (37:24f). When the Jews returned to their own country Zachary promised that they would have a king like David (12:8).

The Chronicler made David the center of his history. The exploits of this victorious soldier, wise ruler, noble king and loyal servant of God were well calculated to fire the hearts of the newly returned exiles with patriotic and religious sentiments (1 Par. 10–29). Ben Sirach, in his praise of the men of old, singles out David for special eulogies (Sir. 47:1–13) because his was "a throne of glory in Israel."

The Evangelists dwell lovingly on the resemblance of Jesus to David. St. John speaks of His birth in the city of David (John 7:42). St. Matthew and St. Luke show in their genealogical tables that Jesus is a descendant of David" (Matt. 1:1 ; Luke 2:4). The people call Him "the son of David" (Matt. 21:9, 15 ; Mark 10:47). St. Peter reminds his brethren that David was a prophet (Acts 2:30). These prophecies are mostly in the Messianic Psalms, which are recited so frequently in the divine office (e.g. 2, 21, 44, 71, 109, etc.). From St. Paul the first Christians learned of Nathan's promise (2 Cor. 6:18 ; Heb. 1:5). In the Apocalypse Jesus' descent from David is one of the last inspired utterances of the Bible (Apoc. 22:16).

Paul Claudel says that every writer comes into the world to say one thing, and if we would understand his life-work we must find what that is and group all else about it. The "one thing" that gives meaning to David's life is summed up in the responsory read on the Tuesday in the seventh week after the octave of Pentecost when, after the account of David's death, we say : "O Lord, if Thy people shall be converted and shall pray in Thy sanctuary, Thou shalt hearken to them and deliver them from the hands of their enemies."

Samuel understood the primacy of the supernatural expressed in these words ; David made it the purpose of his life ; but Saul was never able to adhere to this principle with fixity of purpose. This is one of the lessons that the Church proposes for our consideration, as we re-read in the breviary the story of the successes and the failures of the leaders of God's first kingdom.

THE BOOKS OF KINGS

ON THE seventh Sunday after Pentecost the Church gives us in the liturgy the books of Kings. Each day at matins until the first day of August the lessons of the first nocturn unfold the troubled history of the people of God during the four hundred eventful years between the death of David and the end of the kingdom of Juda. Glory ends in exile because the Jews could not meet the challenge that is expressed in one of the versicles often repeated during these weeks: "Turn to the Lord with all your hearts, put away strange gods. And He will deliver you from the hands of your enemies."

These words contain an important lesson on interior life that St. Madeleine Sophie expressed in her own forceful way: "Interior spirit is the complete sacrifice of self by the mortification of the senses and the conquest of the passions; it is the ever-renewed recollection of the presence of God for whom we act." This is a lesson that only generous and faithful souls can learn, for they alone can turn to God with all their hearts.

The Chosen People forsook the worship of the one true God: they adored the gods of their pagan neighbors. So God delivered the northern part of their kingdom to the Assyrians in 722 B.C. and the southern part of their kingdom to the Babylonians in 586 B.C. The story of the books of Kings is the story of a powerful Jewish state, its division, its decline, its disintegration and fall.

90

Since Pentecost the *mystique* of the liturgy has introduced us to thoughts about the kingdom of Christ which has been presented in the breviary through images drawn from the Old Testament history of the kingdom of God. This is a prophetic vision of the fortunes of the members of the Church of every century; it is the story of our opportunities for victory, our compromises with the enemy, our continual warfare with the powers of darkness, our triumphs and our defeats. The books of Samuel described the establishment and the extension of the kingdom: Samuel, the great unifier of Israel anointed the first two kings, Saul and David, and inaugurated the golden age of the Jewish people (1st–6th week after Pentecost). The books of Kings open with David's last days and the brilliance of Solomon's reign. They close with the bare statement of the plight of a prisoner in Babylon, Joachin, who was the last king of Juda, and the description of the flight of "all the people both little and great" from the land given them by God — a fitting punishment for their centuries of disobedience and idolatry. The eclipse is not total. The kingdom of David has been destroyed — but not forever. "The divine mercies are new every morning." On the last pages of the fourth book of Kings two hopeful signs are recorded: the royal prisoner is treated generously by his captors; and although only a small fraction of the once great nation has survived — still, it has survived. And God can work wonders with very small things.

1 AND 2 KINGS OR 3 AND 4 KINGS

It must sometimes perplex people that Christians of other denominations know certain books of the Bible by names that differ from those used by Catholics. For example, in some Bibles the books that are the subject of this study are known as the first and second books of Kings, whereas in many Catholic versions they are known as the third and fourth books of Kings. A curious story lies behind this difference of name and it takes us back to the second century before Christ. By this time many Jews had made their home in Egypt and were no longer able to read the language of Moses. A new translation had to be prepared for them which came to be known as the *Septuagint*. This Greek word which means "seventy" was given to this translation because of a legend that it was the work of some seventy scribes who came to Alexandria from Jerusalem to translate the Hebrew Bible into Greek. Be that as it may, the translators took the Hebrew *Book of Kings* — once a single volume — and arbitrarily divided it into two almost equal parts, naming them the third and fourth *Kingdoms* because they continue the

history begun in the first and second *Kingdoms* (the books of Samuel).
A further change in title came when Saint Jerome in his Latin transla-
tion, the Vulgate, called the first and the second books of Samuel and
the first and second books of Kings of the Hebrew Bible, the first,
second, third and fourth books of Kings, from the opening word of the
Hebrew text, *Vehammelek,* which means "And the king." Most
English Catholic translations have followed the example of Saint
Jerome in this.

It is the meaning and messages of what appears in the breviary as the
third and fourth books of Kings that we will now examine.

CONTENTS

The books of Kings open with the dramatic plots and counterplots that
darkened David's last years. The most ambitious of his many sons
schemed to succeed him. To put an end to shocking palace intrigues he
ordered Nathan the prophet and Sadoc the priest to anoint Solomon.
The handsome young prince was acclaimed by the people; he was en-
throned in a sumptuous ceremony and was given the homage of the
experienced counselors who had helped to make David a victorious
leader, an efficient ruler, and a well-loved king. The long account of
Solomon's reign is given in the form of a triptych: first, an attractive
picture of the wise sovereign; then, the splendid picture of the magnificent builder; finally, the tragic picture of an idolatrous, pleasure-
loving old man. For the sake of David, his father, and "the man after
God's own heart," the divine chastisements were delayed until the
reign of Solomon's son and successor, Roboam. Shortly after Solomon's
death Jeroboam, another son, made himself the head of the ten tribes
of the Northern Kingdom of Samaria. The Southern Kingdom of Juda,
composed of the tribes of Juda and later, part of the tribe of Benjamin,
followed Roboam and they alone remained faithful to Yahweh. Political division and religious schism separated the Chosen People until
the destruction of Jerusalem in the sixth century before Christ.

The history of the two kingdoms is related in a succession of royal
biographies which tell a synchronized story of the centuries between the
days of Jeroboam and the days of Osee, the first and the last of the
northern kings (3 Kgs. 12–4 Kgs. 17). For more than one hundred and
thirty years the Judeans continued their national existence. The vicissitudes of the surviving Southern Kingdom are described in the lives
of the last Davidic rulers (2 Kgs. 18–25).

The author follows a definite plan in the biography of each monarch:

1. An introductory formula gives the date of the reign, its length, the contemporary ruler in the neighboring kingdom;
2. An appraisal of the character of the king;
3. A documentary citation;
4. A statement of his death and the name of his successor;
5. Miscellaneous facts are sometimes interpolated, for instance, the age of the king, the name of his mother, the place of his burial, etc.

The account of Abiam, a king of Juda, is typical:

Now in the eighteenth year of the reign of Jeroboam the son of Nabat, Abiam reigned over Juda. He reigned three years in Jerusalem. The name of his mother was Maacha . . . And he walked in all the sins of his father . . . His heart was not perfect with the Lord his God, as was the heart of David . . . And the rest of the words of Abiam, and all that he did, are they not written in the chronicles of the kings of Juda? . . . Abiam slept with his fathers and they buried him in the city of David, and Osa his son reigned in his stead (cf. 3Kgs. 15:1–8).

Twice this pattern is deliberately abandoned, once through the insertion of the stories of the fiery Elias (3 Kgs. 17:19; 21) and later through the addition of the adventure of his loyal disciple Eliseus (4 Kgs. 2; 3:4–8:15; 13:14–21). These accounts are closely interwoven with events of national history and with stirring tales of conflict with false prophets (4 Kgs. 20 and 22).

PURPOSE

The aim of the author was primarily religious, not political. He drew upon abundant sources near at hand to show how Yahweh rewarded obedient service with prosperity, and punished sin with suffering. The fate of the Hebrew nation depended upon its observance of the Law of Moses and the worship of the one God, so there are many references to the Temple, its construction and dedication under Solomon, its repeated losses through pillage. Detailed accounts are given of the regulations for its upkeep that were designed by Joas, the changes introduced by Achaz, the profanations of Manasses, the purifications ordered by Josias.

Each king, therefore, was judged not according to the rôle he played

in Near East power politics but according to his attitude to religion. For
this reason the lives of the kings of Juda who were outstanding in their
service of God, and the unhappy reigns of the kings of Israel who were
notorious for their idolatry are described at great length. Many facts,
for example, are recorded of Solomon, the founder of the Temple;
Jeroboam, the instigator of the schism; Achab, who was the worst of the
kings of Israel; Ezechias and Josias, the prayerful reformers of Juda.

Others receive the barest recognition. For example: more than one
recent archaeological expedition in the Near East has added to our
knowledge of the reign of Omri. He was an able ruler of the Northern
Kingdom, successful in his foreign relations, efficient in his conduct of
internal affairs; yet the third book of Kings ignores all this, merely
reporting his change of capital from Therea to Samaria and summing
up the significant years of his reign with the words, "he did evil in the
sight of the Lord" (3 Kgs. 16: 23–28). Clearly the author was not to
be lured away from his original religious purpose by interesting foreign
alliances or "secular" matters, however much future military or political or economic historians might regret his reticence.

This reverence for the Law and the fierce denunciation of all that
was opposed to purity of worship reminds us of Jeremias, who has been
suggested as the author of pages so characteristic of his spirit. Whoever
the author may be, we are certain that he was a priest, a resident of
Jerusalem, a patriot, a lover of reform, a sincerely precise scholar and
a man of prayer.

SOURCES

Perhaps it would be more accurate to refer to "the compiler" or "editor"
than to the author of the books of Kings because this tireless and painstaking worker assembled facts from many documents in the telling of
his richly pictured history. He was probably busy during the sixth century integrating three main sources to which he refers at least thirty-
three times: the *Acts of Solomon,* the *Chronicles of the Kings of Juda*
and the *Annals of the Kings of Israel.* Other material at the writer's disposal included histories of the prophets, an account of the construction
of the Temple, the cycles of Elias and Eliseus with all the *mirabilia* of
their eventful struggle against the worship of the Canaanite gods and
the great lessons of their docility to God. In utilizing these different
documents the compiler sometimes borrowed whole passages which he
inserted in his narrative, sometimes he summarized their contents or
he added facts from other manuscripts to round out his own tale.

The influence of the lessons of the book of Deuteronomy is evident on every page of the books of Kings and guided the selection of much of the material. The same profoundly religious attitude is found in both books, the same understanding of the danger of idolatry, the same realization of Yahweh's transcendent love. Sin against so merciful a God is not merely disobedience but the basest form of ingratitude. There are dark shadows that deepen ominously as we reach the climax of this history — the fall of Jerusalem and the beginning of the exile — but there is also hope. The words of Deuteronomy are not heard but their message lingers like a remembered melody: "If with all your heart you seek the Lord you will truly find Him" (cf. Deut. 4:29).

THREE GREAT KINGS

So much for the books of Kings in general. Are there any clues as to the important lessons we ought to learn as we study the contrasting portraits of these long dead rulers? Let us turn to the last chapters of the book of Ecclesiasticus. There we find a summary of the deeds of Israel's great heroes, "Praise of the Men of Old." No king from the North receives an honorable citation along with Abraham, Moses and Josue; and only two Davidic kings from the South, Ezechias and Josias, are praised with Solomon. A study of these three kings will show us why they were singled out for special honor among all the rulers of Juda and Israel. Just as Solomon is honored for the glory with which he surrounded the worship of Yahweh, so Ezechias is given as a model of trust in divine providence, and Josias is remembered for the zeal with which he rededicated his people to the service of God.

SOLOMON

Sirach, for so the second century B.C. author of Ecclesiasticus is known, sums up Solomon's reign under four headings: the blessings of peace which made it possible for him to build the great Temple, the wisdom that was the wonder of the world, the royal wealth such as the people of God had never known before and "the stain" on all this glory which was caused by his sins (Ecclus. 47:15–26).

Later generations concurred with Sirach's verdict: Solomon began well, "O how wise you were in your youth" (Ecclus. 47:15). Scripture affords abundant evidence that he was an energetic and brilliant ruler and every year archaeologists discover further evidence of his material success. Excavations in many places in Palestine show that his reign was prosperous and that his kingdom was surprisingly modern. At

Megiddo, the strategic fortress-city overlooking the plain of Esdraelon, recent digging has brought to light an immense complex of stables for about 500 horses. This was in but one city in Solomon's chain of defence. There were many more. Here are buildings much like a perfectly planned large-scale modern stock farm and we learn that the king needed horses not only for chariot use but also for horse-trading, which was a successful money-making venture of his days. Gold and silver, silks, spices and jewels were carried from Red Sea and Persian Gulf ports to the harbors of Ezion-geber, which Solomon built on the Gulf of Aqabah where docks and a great smelter have recently been unearthed. All of these archaeological findings corroborate the absolute accuracy of verse after verse of the books of Kings but they added nothing to the king's spiritual stature. Records of his inner life are meagre and latter generations were to remember David who planned the Temple rather than Solomon who built it. Notice the last verse of the account of the dedication as we find it in the third book of Kings: "The people returned home rejoicing and glad in heart for all the good things that the Lord had done for David His servant and Israel His people" (3 Kgs. 8:66).

Without peace, much of this material splendor would not have been possible but Solomon's success is also attributable to his wisdom. This was God's gift to him at the beginning of his reign when he asked for and received the wisdom for which he was famed. The wisdom he sought was the power of ruling with justice and of judging with prudence. This gift was given him with such divine generosity that it was said he "exceeded all the kings on the earth in riches and wisdom" (3 Kgs. 10:23). His name was always to be associated with every type of "wisdom literature" in Israel, just as the Law is associated with Moses, and the psalms are attributed to David. But as an inspired writer Solomon never reached the spiritual heights that David made so easily his own.

Through his justice and good government, through his peace and prosperity, through the magnificence with which he surrounded God's worship, Solomon ranks as one of the great kings of Israel and of the world. His most attractive qualities and his glorious achievements have won him the privilege of prefiguring the person of the Messias and His works. But the splendid promise of the early years of this prince of peace never seem to have been fulfilled. Saint Augustine notes sadly that Scripture records for us no act of repentance for the king's sins of polygamy and idolatry and he fears that this silence has an ominous meaning. Holiness from the first grace until the last is God's gift. "May He who began the good work in you perfect the same" is the prayer the Church places on our lips in order to remind us that God is both the beginning and end of our sanctification. In the Apocalypse He tells us: "I am the Alpha and the Omega, the first and the last, the beginning and the end" (22:13).

What Sirach calls "the stain" on all this glory was Solomon's failure to live up to his first ideals. His advantageous marriages with foreign princesses, his profitable trade with distant lands, even his reputation for wisdom brought pagans and pagan ideas into the Holy Land. These "germs of death" lowered the spiritual ideals of the People of God and were the immediate cause of the schism which was to divide the country at his death.

EZECHIAS

Sirach also taught the Jews to reverence the memory of Ezechias because this king "did that which pleased God and walked valiantly in the way of David his father" (Ecclus. 49:25). "Trust Yahweh" is one of the great lessons of his life. He taught this truth by his example during a moment of national peril. "Israel, unlike another nation, cannot seek help from any political alliance," so the deep-souled prophet Isaias twice admonished the king when Assyrian forces under Sennacherib conquered most of western Asia and lay siege to Jerusalem.

The interest of the biblical account (4 Kgs. 18–19; Isa. 36–38) is heightened by a comparison with the account of the crisis as recorded in Assyrian annals:

> As for Ezechias the Judean, he did not submit to my yoke. I laid siege to 46 of his strong cities, walled forts and to the countless small villages in the vicinity . . . the king himself I made prisoner in Jerusalem, his royal residence, like a bird in a cage.

The Assyrians, despite the king's bold tone, did not take Jerusalem. A plague made imperative the immediate evacuation of Sennacherib's army, or to quote the words of the author of the book of Kings:

> And it came to pass that night, that an angel of the Lord came, and slew in the camp of the Assyrians a hundred and eighty-five thousand. And when Ezechias arose early in the morning he saw all the bodies of the dead. And Sennacherib departing went away (4 Kgs. 19:35f).

Ezechias deserved his chronicler's divinely inspired praise: "He trusted in the Lord the God of Israel . . . wherefore the Lord was with him" (cf. 4 Kgs. 18:5–7). Like saints of every age he knew that God's mercy is eternal, so eternal, too, must be our trust.

The occasion of the king's heroic act of trust has attracted the attention of poets, historians and artists. Byron begins his story of God's providential intervention on behalf of His people with the lines:

> The Assyrian came down like the wolf on the fold,
> And his cohorts were gleaming with purple and gold;
> And the sheen of their spears was like stars on the sea,
> When the blue waves roll nightly on deep Galilee.

Herodotus, the father of history, in the second book of his masterpiece describes the haste and confusion of the Assyrian defeat, while Rubens has made immortal the moment of flight on a canvas that is vibrant with movement and agitation. The angel of the Lord leans from a thunderous sky, majestic horses rear in uncontrolled fury and terror; the horror of the dead, the agony of the dying make this painting an unforgettable commentary on 4 Kgs. 19:35.

JOSIAS

Josias was the most devout of all the Jewish kings. Sirach has words of gentle praise for a ruler everyone loved: his memory is like a fragrant perfume, like sweet honey, like music at a banquet of wine (Ecclus. 49:1f). The Jews had, at his accession, been long accustomed to scandals at court. Ammon, the pious king's father, "had trespassed more and more;" Manasses, his grandfather, was "the most profane of all the line of David," but of Josias we read "while he was yet young he began to seek after the God of David."

In a scene that recalls the first time the Israelites assembled at the foot of Mount Sinai to hear the Ten Commandments (Ex. 19), Josias gathered his people together in the Temple and they listened to a solemn reading of Deuteronomy, a book of the Bible containing the words of Moses (4 Kgs. 23). Exultant prayer and praise followed the sacred reading both in the desert and in the Holy City. And the great ceremony concluded on both occasions with the formal renewal of the covenant of the alliance through a fervent celebration of the Paschal sacrifice. Father Louis Bouyer in his classic *Liturgical Piety* offers persuasive evidence that this primitive covenant with all its ceremonial ritual was a figure of "the new and eternal covenant" repeated daily on our altars and to be everlastingly realised in the heavenly Jerusalem.

Unfortunately the renewal under Josias was to be of short duration and the Lord had to tell His faithful servant that the Jews would be punished for their idolatry but

Because your heart was tender and you have humbled yourself before the Lord . . . I will gather you to your fathers in peace so that your eyes will not see all the evils that I will bring upon this place (cf. 4 Kgs. 19:16–20).

So the reign of the last king of David's line came to an end. His successors were never to rule as independent sovereigns. He had been the most eminent of the reforming kings of Juda, so Newman was able to say with perfect truth: "Here we have the pattern of reformers: singleness of heart, gentleness of temper, in the midst of zeal resoluteness, and decision in action." We understand why at his death "all Juda and Jerusalem and particularly Jeremias mourned for him" (2 Par. 35:24).

FURTHER READING

So brief a summary of the forty-seven chapters of the third and fourth books of Kings cannot give an adequate understanding of their variety and interest. Nor can the lessons of the breviary read during the summer months or the excerpts found in the epistles of some Lenten Masses suffice. Additional and recommended reading should include details about:

Solomon's wisdom . . . . 3 Kgs. 3:1–28
The dedication of the Temple . . . . 3 Kgs. 8:1–66
Roboam's rashness . . . . 3 Kgs. 12:1–33
Achab and the prophet Elias . . . . 3 Kgs. 17:1 — 18:46
The last days of Elias . . . . 4 Kgs. 1:1 — 2:18
The wonders worked by Eliseus . . . . 4 Kgs. 4:1 — 8:6
Jehu's reign . . . . 4 Kgs. 9:1 — 10:36
The reform of Joas . . . . 4 Kgs. 12:1–21
The fall of the Northern Kingdom . . . . 4 Kgs. 17:1–41
The days of Ezechias . . . . 4 Kgs. 18:1 — 20:21
The reforms of Josias . . . . 4 Kgs. 22:1 — 23:30
Jerusalem sacked . . . . 4 Kgs. 25:1–30

THE LESSON OF THE BOOKS OF KINGS

Hesed is a Hebrew word rich in meaning and difficult to translate. No single English equivalent can convey the goodness, mercy, long-suffering, patience, kindness and clemency that invest this word with such beauty and power when it is used in the Old Testament to tell us of

God's love for man. This one word contains the lesson of the books of Kings. Centuries before the Chosen People had made their home in Palestine, Yahweh had used similar words when He testified to Moses on Mount Sinai: "The Lord God is merciful and gracious, patient and of much compassion and true" (Ex. 34:6). The long history of the books of Kings affords compelling evidence on every page that the Lord shows mercy to them that love Him. Disobedience, ingratitude, unbelief on the part of men are met with God's forgiveness, new proofs of His graciousness, fresh evidence of His love: and this, not once, but many times. In this way men's hearts were prepared for the greatest gift of all, the coming of another David, the King of Kings, in the days of the New Covenant. The *hesed* of the Old Testament becomes the *agape* of the New and the ultimate lesson of life is, in the words of Saint John, that "God is love."

The books of Kings show us a kingdom that did not endure yet prefigured, in the mystery of God's wisdom, the kingdom of the Son of His Love which the liturgy of the feast of Christ the King tells us will be: "a kingdom eternal and universal, a kingdom of truth and life, a kingdom of holiness and grace, a kingdom of justice, love and peace." It is for this that we ask when we pray: "Thy kingdom come."

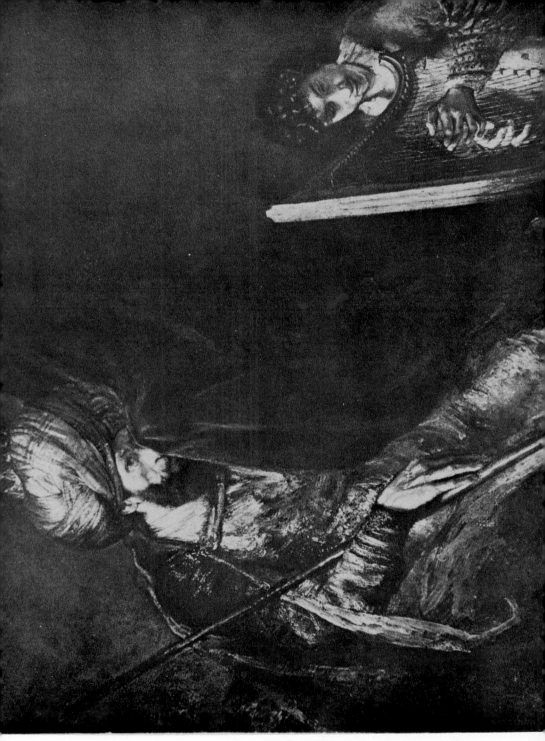

SAUL AND DAVID, Rembrandt, 1650–
1660, The Hague, Mauritshuis, p. 87.

THE ANGEL LEAVING TOBIAS AND HIS
FAMILY, Rembrandt, 1637, Paris, Louvre, p. 121.

JUDITH, Carlo Saraceni, 1610–
1620, Vienna, Museum, p. 130.

THE BURIAL OF THE COUNT ORGAZ, El
Greco, 1586, Toledo, Church of San Tome, p. 145.

PARALIPOMENA

THE books of Paralipomena are the last books of the Hebrew Bible. There they are called "the events of the days," a title to which St. Jerome took exception, declaring that it would have been more correct to call them "a chronicle of the events of the whole of sacred history" because the first chapter opens with Adam and the last chapter closes with the decree of Cyrus that put an end to the Babylonian captivity in 536 B.C. and allowed the Jews to return to their own country.

Martin Luther agreed with St. Jerome on this point and in English Protestant Bibles, today, these books are called Chronicles. In English Catholic Bibles they are called Paralipomena, a name borrowed from the Greek, meaning "the book of things omitted." This, too, is an appropriate title because in these chapters are many facts not recorded in the books of Kings, to which they are, in a certain sense, the complement. But neither title gives an idea of the full scope of the book.

VISION . . . COURAGE . . . TRUST

This summary of sacred history was made, it seems, about two hundred years before the birth of Christ, by a Levite of Jerusalem. He is called the Chronicler. The temple was the center of his life, which moved according to the double rhythm of service and praise. These were the difficult days after the exile. Juda had lost its independence and was now only part of a province of a vast empire. The people were disheartened.

101

The remembrance of past glories might help them, the Chronicler thought. Historical books they already had in abundance, as is evident from the sources to which he refers: "books" of monarchs, "acts" of prophets, "words," "records," "annals." So, making use of thirteen of these non-canonical sources and drawing largely from Deuteronomy and other inspired books, he set about his work.

To David he gave a place of pre-eminence, not for his own sake, but because he was the head of the house from which the Messias was to come. He made clear the importance of David's legislation for the Levites. The duties Moses had assigned them in the wilderness were now replaced with more priestly functions. He showed the importance of and the need for a renewal and restoration of the Davidic ideal. This, he believed, would give the people vision, courage, trust.

Vision, he felt would be theirs, if he showed them the theocracy of David and urged them to support the temple and observe the Law. Courage, he hoped would be theirs, if he showed them, with historic examples, that God abandons only those who abandon Him. Trust, he was sure would be theirs, if he showed them that God is the God of history and that He is guiding the destinies of men and nations to their appointed ends.

HIGH AMBITION AND DEEDS THAT SURPASS IT

The Chronicler's purpose explains many anomalies in his book. True history, for him, begins with David, so the history up to the time of Saul is given in short, occasionally annotated, genealogies. To Saul himself is allotted no more than eleven verses. While Newman, reading the many chapters in the books of Kings that show Saul's "high ambition and deeds which surpass it, fame crowning them all," can list five reasons why Saul failed, the Chronicler briefly refers to his disobedience and his lack of trust. Newman regrets that many men, like Saul, forget that their distress comes from God and that God will remove it in His own way, if they are steadfast.

Others, too, are impatient in times of testing; or wish to serve God in their own way, not His; or, are willing to bear part of the trial God puts on them, but then fall away; or, keep the letter of God's laws grudgingly and cold-heartedly because, like the king, they are wanting in love.

The Chronicler pauses for none of these analyses of Saul's failure or for descriptions of the incidents on which they are based. His summary is simple and succinct: "To death the Lord doomed Saul, and passed on his kingdom to David the son of Jesse."

DAVID THE LITURGIST AND THEOCRATIC KING

To understand the life of David it is necessary to read the chapters in the books of Kings that record his life as well as those in the books of Paralipomena. The contrast between the two accounts is instructive.

The Chronicler is obviously not interested in all the incidents of the reign of the king whose divinely chosen dynasty is the subject of the rest of his book and according to whose spirit he wishes all men to live. He does not give us David the monarch or David the military man; in fact he refers readers interested only in history to the books of Kings, whereas he concentrates on David the liturgist, David the lover of the Law: the man who selected the site for the temple, prepared its blue prints, arranged for the transfer of the ark of the covenant, listed the duties of the Levites, organized the ceremonial, looked after the music, taught the singers their tasks, and composed some sacred chants still sung to honor God today.

It is the Chronicler's picture of David the theocratic king that shows us why he is great among the rulers of the earth. To be perfectly frank, David was merely a petty kinglet of an insignificant state. He had no cosmic stature by human standards and to judge him by these standards is to miss the measure of his greatness. He is the king divinely chosen to rule in God's name. In him the promises made to Abraham are fulfilled. His sovereignty was to be undisturbed, his throne, to endless time, secure.

The Chronicler slowly and lovingly traced the lines of this portrait. No detail was too trivial if it would inspire the people with respect and love for the ruler "after God's own heart."

THE GOLDEN AGE

But David could only make plans, provide materials for the temple and lay down the duties of its ministers — the realization of all this was left to his son Solomon. The Chronicler's singleness of purpose is evident in the nine chapters devoted to this unhappy ruler. No mention is made of his idolatry and his many failings; for these facts the Chronicler refers his reader to other sources. Primacy of place is given to all that concerns the temple: its construction, the king's prayer at the dedication and the promises God then made.

Later generations were to look back to the golden age when Israel, under Saul, David and Solomon, was united for the only time in history. They would deplore the greed and secular ambition that was responsible for the rebellion that followed Solomon's death and led to the division and eventually the loss of their country.

The Chronicler has not time for such a study. He holds up a mirror to the past and shows his contemporaries that Israel was great when it was faithful to God, when it obyed the Law and when it worshipped God in the sanctuary He had chosen. He wished his people to become holy so that in them the promises made to David might be fulfilled.

MEN MOST LIKE DAVID

Similar principles control the Chronicler's treatment of the other kings of Juda. He singles out for special attention men most like David in their love of the temple, in their opposition to idolatry, in their whole-hearted service of the Lord. He shows that when they trusted God, He never failed them; and when they trusted in themselves, they failed in all they did. To one bound by God's alliance, alliances with princes, no matter how powerful, could little avail.

These lessons the Chronicler makes specially clear in his account of the reigns of five out of the twenty kings who succeeded Solomon on Juda's throne. These kings are Asa, Josaphat, Joas, Josias, Ezechias.

A FOOL'S PART

Asa's reign, we are shown, contains in miniature the lessons of Paralipomena. His first years were fervently religious and his country was prosperous and at peace. Never an idol was left in the land, the Lord's altar was dedicated anew, solemnly the covenant was ratified. False worship was prosecuted without fear or favor. Even the royal mother was deprived of her queenly dignity when she built a forest shrine.

Then Asa forsook the Lord, and, as he had been warned by Azarias the prophet, he found himself forsaken. "Thou hast played the fool's part," the prophet told Asa when he had called the king of Syria to his aid. "Wide as earth is the Lord's scrutiny, and there he gives mastery where he finds hearts that have utter faith in him." Asa was not one of these. Even in his last illness, the Chronicler tells, he did not "have recourse to the Lord, trusting rather in the skill of physicians"; and so the account of his reign closes with these laconic words: "dying, he was laid to rest."

FOR FEW CAN GOD ALONE SUFFICE

Josaphat, rich and renowned, is the second of David's successors to merit a detailed history of his reign. The reason is obvious: a ruler who could tell his people: "Trust in the Lord your God, and you have nothing to fear; trust his prophets, and all shall go well with you," was surely a ruler according to the Chronicler's ideal.

When Josaphat followed his own advice, his country was secure and for years on all his borders there was peace. When the three great enemies, the Ammonites, the Edomites, the Moabites attacked, he wisely turned to the Lord with the words: "It is for thee, our God, to grant redress; we have no strength of our own to meet such an onslaught as this; despairing hearts, that know not where else to turn, we turn to thee."

On that occasion victory was his, as it always is when our whole trust is in God. But Josaphat was no wiser than are we. Few are the souls for whom God alone can suffice. Scheme and plot he must to win the support of the evilly ruling Ochozias of Israel. Together they would build a fleet and send it to Tharsis.

The vessels started on the long journey. Then the prophet summed up the results of the king's misplaced trust in these words: "The Lord has shattered those hopes of thine, because of thy alliance with Ochozias; and the ships were wrecked before ever they reached Tharsis." There were other failures and other successes in his life. The failures, the people forgot and when he died they chose to remember only that he was "a king who had set his whole heart in following the Lord."

GLADLY THEY COME WITH THEIR GIFTS

When we come across the words "Now Joas had a mind to put the Lord's house in repair," we know that we have found another king in whom the Chronicler will take great interest. Little mention is made of the six years' reign of his aunt Athalia (she was not of the house of David) or of the incidents that Racine so skillfully combined in his drama that related the overthrow of the usurping queen and the coronation of Joas, the young prince. Nor are the facts given that the French dramatist summed up in the closing lines of his play:

> In heaven kings find a judge most severe,
> The sinless and orphans a Father most dear.

But so much is said in Paralipomena of the king's zeal in collecting money for the temple restoration that he merits the attention of those in need of development funds in any age. The account of his successful drive is heartening to those engaged in similar campaigns. The Chronicler relates:

> Gladly did chieftains and common folk together come with their gifts for the Lord's treasury, piling the chest high till it was full. When the Levites saw that a great sum was amassed, it was time they should take it into the royal presence . . . together they poured out the money that was in the chest, which they then put back in its place. Every day this was done, and the great sum collected was paid to the master-builders . . . (2 Par. 24).

Although the drive exceeded its goal, its lesson was lost on King Joas. Joaida, the high priest, who had crowned him when he was only seven and had guided him during the first thirty years of his reign, died. With his death, the temple was forgotten and Zacharias, the prophet who dared reproach Joas, was stoned there where he stood in the temple court. So many misdeeds marked the last ten years of his life that he was not buried with Juda's other kings. Once again the Chronicler has illustrated his theme: right-doing is blessed, calamities befall those who fail to persevere.

RIGHT DOING IS BLESSED

It is only the first part of this theme that could be used as a title for the four chapters (2 Par. 29–32) describing the reign of Ezechias. The Chronicler's account opens with the highly favorable comment, "Here was one that obeyed the Lord's will no less than his father David before him," and closes on the same note: "In all that he did, he prospered," adding that on one occasion when God had left him to his own counsel, "it was but to try him and test the disposition of his heart."

NEVER SWERVING TO RIGHT OR LEFT

No better model could have been offered the post-exilic Jews for the loyal and generous observance of the Law than the reign of Ezechias and his great grandson Josias who was "obedient to the Lord's will and followed the example of his ancestor, King David, never swerving to right or left."

Reform was necessary when he came to the throne and Newman points out that many a man who did all that Josias had done would have prided himself on his achievement and become self-willed, self-confident and hard-hearted. But like all those who know the lessons of *The Way of Divine Love*, Josias took no credit to himself and gave all the glory to the Lord.

He was the last independent sovereign of David's house and the Chronicler makes it clear that on him had descended the zeal and loyalty which had made the son of Jesse "a man after God's own heart."

A LAUGHING STOCK

True friendship, St. Jerome believed, could find no firmer foundation than "a common fear of God and a joint study of the divine Scriptures." He wished those he loved to know each book of the Bible and he painstakingly prepared them to profit from their study of the inspired pages. To a new friend he has this to say about the necessity of reading Paralipomena:

> The book of things omitted or epitome of the Old Dispensation is of such importance and value that without it anyone who should claim for himself a knowledge of the Scriptures would become a laughing stock. . . .

Then he explains that this book cannot be read without reference to the rest of the Bible because much that is in it "serves to throw light on narratives passed over in the books of Kings and upon questions suggested in the Gospel." The following recommended readings are an attempt to follow the Saint's suggestion. To those who take his advice may come the reward the Saint promised his friend: "I beg of you," he writes, "to live among these books, to meditate upon them, to know nothing else, to seek nothing else. Does not such a life seem to you a foretaste of heaven here on earth?"

PASSAGES OMITTED IN THE BOOKS OF KINGS

"Does this thought come from God?". . . . . .1 Par. 13:1–4
"Here, said David, is the Lord's home". . . . . .1 Par. 22:1–19
"Then David handed Solomon the full plan of
  porch and temple". . . . . .1 Par. 28:1–29:30
"The spirit of the Lord moved Azarias". . . . . .2 Par. 15:1–19
"Josaphat reigned and the Lord was with him". . . . . . .2 Par. 17:1–19
"It is for thee, our God, to grant redress". . . . . .2 Par. 20:7–30

PASSAGES THROWING LIGHT ON GOSPEL QUESTIONS

"Overseers of the sanctuary". . . . . .Luke 1:5; 1 Par. 24:1–17
"Each man was to pay the tax". . . . .Matt. 17:24–27; 2 Par. 24:1–5
"They stoned Zacharias". . . . . . .Matt. 23:33–39; 2 Par. 24:15–22

108

"Befriending the captives"........Luke 10:25–37; 2 Par. 28:9–15
"They desecrated the sanctuary" Matt. 23:34–36; 2 Par. 26:14–16

OUR LIFE IS A PARENTHESIS

Interesting as is the Saint's suggestion, it in no way conveys the complete message of the book, for Paralipomena is more than a history and its philosophy of history is well worth our attention.

Archbishop Ireland used to say that if St. Paul returned to earth, he would return as a journalist. Perhaps it might be said with equal truth that were the Chronicler to apply for a position on the faculty of a twentieth century university, he would ask to join the history department and lecture on the philosophy of history. For this position his books of Paralipomena, Esdras and Nehemias (of which he is also believed to have been the author) would seem to qualify him, and those who signed up for his courses would soon discover that he is a theologian as well as an historian.

His historical angle of vision is not limited to dimensions of space and time. History, in his eyes, is not meant merely to amplify our knowledge of the past or satisfy our intellectual curiosity. History, in his eyes, gives us a vision of God's creation, moving from God who is its origin to God who is its goal. He would have agreed with John Donne who said that "Our whole life is but a *parenthesis*, our *receiving* of our soule, and *delivering* it back againe, makes up the perfect sentence."

It is to recapture this spirit that we reread the book today. The community who lived near the Dead Sea and about whom we are learning more each year was inspired by the Chronicler's ideal; they tried to measure up to his moral demands and model their lives on his reverence for the Law. The early Christian communities converted by Paul whom we meet in the Acts and to whom the epistles were addressed had been nurtured in the Chronicler's teaching.

It is this insight that makes the book valuable for us rather than its use in our liturgical books. Occasional verses appear as antiphons in the breviary. On Monday at Lauds there is a canticle from this book (1 Par. 29:10–13) and some of its verses are used in the beautiful offertory of the Mass for the dedication of a church. In them we find the acknowledgment of God's dominion that pervades all that the Chronicler has written:

My God, Thou readest our hearts, I know it well, and it is the honest heart Thou lovest. With honesty of intent I have made all these offerings gladly, and gladly have I seen all that are assembled make their gifts to Thee (1 Par. 29:17f.).

THOU ART THE OVERLORD

When Cesar Franck was a boy at school he won as a prize a copy of the Gospels that his family was to treasure long after his death. Its carefully worn pages are a proof of this great composer's love of the inspired word and the often handled chapters 5–7 of St. Matthew's Gospel testify to his life-long preoccupation with the Sermon on the Mount. Not until his last years did he attempt a musical composition based on the charter of the New Law with its simple radiant figure of the God-Man, sublime and compassionate, omnipotent and tender, the father of the world to come, the prince bringing peace. It is this divine figure with a message of salvation won through love that gives unity to *The Beatitudes*, one of the most simple and moving of all oratorios.

Had the devout old man made a similar study of the Old Law, he might have enriched the world with still another musical masterpiece. Here, too, a single figure would unify the composition, the figure of a God, "the God of our fathers," "great above all gods," as the Chronicler portrays Him, one "whom heaven itself, and the heaven above the heavens cannot contain" (2 Par. 2:26), yet who heeds every plea for protection, loves the poor and the weak, sends victory and defeat, raises up kings and destroys nations, and to whom we can pray in David's words:

> Blessed art Thou, O Lord the God of our father Israel,
> From the beginning to the end of time.
> Thine, Lord, the magnificence . . .
> Splendor and glory and majesty are Thine . . .
> Of all princes, Thou art the overlord (1 Par. 29:10–12).

To read history mindful of this Overlord is to see God at work in the world and in our lives. But we have been warned that to see God is to die. To what must we die? To all that is selfish and narrow and distrustful. To all that prevents God from freely working out in us and through us His perfect will. It was to win men to this vision of God that the Chronicler set down things that had been omitted until his day.

THE BOOKS OF ESDRAS
AND NEHEMIAS

IN THE oldest Hebrew Bibles the books of Esdras and Nehemias formed one entitled "The Book of Esdras." It is believed to have been edited by "The Chronicler", the reverent lover of Yahweh, who recapitulated in the books of Paralipomena the history of the people of God from creation until the end of the Babylonian exile. Vocabulary and style bear out this claim, as do the inclusion of documents, genealogies and long lists of names. Central in both works is the desire to show the beauty of the divine plan, the importance of divine worship and the fidelity with which God keeps His promises. It is on this note that the book of Esdras opens in the year 538:

In the first year of the Persian king, Cyrus, the Lord fulfilled the promise which He had made through Jeremias. He put a new resolve into the heart of Cyrus, king of Persia, who thereupon published a written decree all through his dominions; A message, it said, from Cyrus, king of Persia. The Lord God of heaven has made me master of the world, and now He will have me rebuild His own temple for Him at Jerusalem, a city of Judaea. Who is left among you of that race? To Jerusalem let him go, in Judaea, with divine aid to speed him; and there let him help to build the temple of the Lord God of Israel, who is the true God. And let all others take note, that such a man is to receive assistance from his neighbours; silver and gold, stores and beasts are to be put at his disposal, apart from the offerings they make, of their own free will, to this temple of God at Jerusalem (1:1–4).

110

The recently emancipated Jews faced three big challenges: the long journey to Jerusalem, the discouragement due to the apparent failure of their best efforts, and the difficulty of building the temple. That all three challenges were met and victoriously answered is largely due to the five men whom God chose to lead His people in these difficult years. Three of them are praised by Ecclesiasticus:

The fame of *Zorobabel* what words of ours shall enhance? The jewel God wore on His right hand for signet ring; he with *Josue* son of Josedec, rebuilt God's house that then lay ruined; raised up a holy temple of the divine glory the eternal dwelling-place. Nor shall *Nehemias* be soon forgotten, that mended these ruined walls of ours, our gates built and barred, our homes restored to us (49:13-15).

Two prophets, *Aggeus* and *Zacharias*, heartened the repatriates and the example of *Esdras* is held in such veneration that Jews honor him today as the founder of modern Judaism.

THE FIRST ZIONISTS

The exact sequence of events is difficult to determine. Here we will follow the order as given in the Bible, as the following reading plan indicates:

The book of Esdras

Part I. Zorobabel leads the Jews to Jerusalem
1. The edict of Cyrus (1:1–11)
2. The construction of the altar (3:1–6)
3. The rebuilding of the temple (3:7 – 6:15)
4. The dedication of the temple (6:16–22)

Part II. Esdras leads the Jews to Jerusalem
1. The return (7:1–8:36)
2. The correction of abuses (9:1–10:40)

The book of Nehemias

Part III. Nehemias rebuilds the walls of Jerusalem
1. The situation (1:1–2:20)
2. The task accomplished (3:1–6:19)

Part IV. Religious Reforms of Esdras and Nehemias
1. The renewal of the covenant (8:1–10:39)
2. The dedication of the walls (12:27–42)
3. The provision made for priests (12:43–46)
4. The correction of abuses (13:1–31)

Many Jews resolved to make the three or four month journey across the desert to Jerusalem when they learned of Cyrus' decree, although some of the more successful exiles elected to remain in Babylon. The archives of the flourishing city of Nippur contain the names of wealthy Jewish bankers who were among the leading financiers of the Persian empire when their brethren were struggling to restore the glory of Israel. The more spiritual among them praised God for His fidelity to His promises, so clear was it to all that the words of the prophets had been fulfilled. In 605 when the glory of the house of David had grown dim and the shadow of exile had darkened the land, Jeremias brought this message from the Lord to the people of Jerusalem: "For seventy years this whole land shall be a desert and a portent, and the King of Babylon shall have all these peoples for his slaves" (25:14).

The seventy years of servitude had passed and the conqueror in his turn was conquered. According to the first century Jewish historian, Josephus, Cyrus resolved to issue his decree when he learned that the restoration of the Jews to their own land had been foretold by the prophets. When the powerful Persian ruler read the sacred books of the Jews, he marveled at the divine power and he was seized by a strong desire and ambition to do what had been written. Moreover, he determined to return to Jerusalem "all the vessels of God which King Nabuchodonosor had taken as spoil from the temple and carried off to Babylon". There were, "in all, of gold and silver appurtenances, five thousand four hundred". These he gave to his treasurer, asking that they be kept safely by the Jews until they could be used by the priests in the building to be erected on the same spot where Solomon's temple had once stood.

That this generosity was characteristic of Cyrus is attested by the Rassam Cylinder in the British Museum. This cuneiform text records that he restored statues of gods stolen by Nabonides, king of Babylon, from Mesopotamian shrines. That it was welcome to the Jews can be readily imagined for the plight of the refugees when they reached Palestine after their long journey was pitiable. The first Zionists had much to suffer.

Most families returned to the same plots of land their forefathers had occupied. Merchants and craftsmen preferred to seek their fortunes in Jerusalem. Priests settled in the villages that had been assigned them. Some found that during their absence their land had been claimed and tilled by bedouin who refused to move away. Others sought to increase their holdings. Friction was inevitable but at the end of two months, the leaders, Josue and Zorobabel, ordered that the Law of Moses be observed and burnt-sacrifice regularly offered.

No more than this did they then dare do, with hostile nations threatening them on every side and it was not until a year later that the foundation-stone of the temple was laid amid the laments of older folk who remembered the vanished glory of the first temple (with all the sorrowful memories it evoked) and the rejoicing of the younger people who looked into a future which to them was bright with promise. But not for long.

When the Samaritans (a mixture of peoples brought from all parts of the Assyrian empire and settled in Samaria after Sargon had conquered the Northern Kingdom in 722) were not allowed to share in the construction, they succeeded in having the work stopped. The Jews had not wished these worshippers of Yahweh and idols to help them and this refusal is part of the animosity that was still apparent five centuries later when Jesus sat beside Jacob's well and asked a Samaritan woman for a drink of water.

It was not until Darius came to the Persian throne that the Jews completed their project, spurred on by the words of the prophets Aggeus and Zacharias. What is known about this sanctuary? Very little. The blue print seems to have been similar to that used by Solomon but the structure was far less costly and the furnishings poor. The holy of holies was empty, for the ark of the covenant had disappeared during the exile. On the single stone slab that marked the place where it once stood, the high priest placed his censer each year on the feast of the Atonement. Nor were the ten golden candelabra restored; instead in the holy place stood the golden altar of incense, the table for the showbread and a seven-branched candlestick.

But the work of restoration was not only a matter of rebuilding, it was also a matter of religious reform. The two men divinely chosen were Esdras and Nehemias. So close knit are their names that it is difficult to establish the chronological order of their activity. Nehemias, one of the most noble of Old Testament heroes, opens his memoirs with these words:

ONE HAND FOR WORK, ONE CLOSING ON A SPEAR

"Mercy, I cried, Thou God of heaven, the strong, the great, the terrible! Thou who ever keepest Thy gracious promises to the souls that love Thee, and are true to Thy commandments. . . . Listen to the prayer I offer Thee now."

Nehemias was cupbearer to the Persian king and when he learned of the slow progress made in Jerusalem by those who had returned and of their lax observance of the Law, he resolved to go to their help. He extended the "short absence" the king and queen granted him to a twelve-year stay in the holy city. His first care was to repair the city ramparts, which he found badly damaged, and to replace the gates and towers. His efficiency and drive surmounted every obstacle — the inertia of the Jews, the ridicule of his opponents, the charges of ambition and the false advice of a pseudo-prophet.

Force he met with force. His account of the difficulties gives us the measure of the man and the means he took to triumph over them:

Back we went to our several posts at the wall; and thenceforward the warriors among us were divided into two companies; one of these remained at work, while behind them under the clan chiefs of Juda, the rest stood arrayed for battle, with lance and shield, bow and breastplate. And even while they were at work, built they or loaded or carried loads, it was one hand to work with, and one closing still on a javelin; nor was there ever a workman but must build with his sword girt at his side. And the men that blew the trumpets were close beside me; I had warned nobles and chiefs and common folk, Here is a task for many to do; spread wide apart, we are sundered far here on the wall and there; rally, all of you, to any point where you hear the trumpet sound, and our God will be our speed. We officers too must take our share in the work, only half of us standing by with our spears, from dawn till the stars rise. And to the common folk I said, Each of you, and his manservant with him, must lodge here in Jerusalem itself, taking turn and turn about, day and night. As for myself, and my clansmen and servants, and the men of my bodyguard, we never took our garments off all the while, save when we stripped for washing (Neh. 4:16–23).

THY GOD'S LAW

A new order began for the community when Esdras reached Jerusalem. He was a priest, learned in the Law. At the Persian court he was charged with Jewish affairs and to him the king gave plenipotentiary powers, saying:

It is for thee, Esdras, who dost carry with thee the wise precepts of thy God, to appoint judges and magistrates, that will try the causes of all such persons beyond the river as are acquainted with thy God's law; and such as do not know it, you may instruct freely. If anyone neglects to observe that law, or the king's law either, these judges shall have power to pronounce sentence on him of death, exile, confiscation of his goods, or imprisonment (1 Esdras 7:25–26).

The Law of Moses was now placed on an equal footing with the law of the state. Both Esdras and Nehemias exacted respectful obedience from officials and people. Mixed marriages were regulated. The sabbath and the sabbatical year were to be faithfully observed. Offerings and fuel for sacrifice were prescribed, first fruits and tithes were specified. The Law was read and explained to the people. Feasts were solemnly observed. One of the few occasions when liturgical use is made of the book of Esdras and Nehemias is the Mass of Ember Wednesday in September when the account is read of the celebration of the pasch (2 Esdras 8:1–10). For the great achievements of both Esdras and Nehemias ought we to repeat the final plea with which the Chronicler's history of the restoration closes: "Not unremembered, my God, be all this, not unrewarded."

THREE CHALLENGES

What lessons have their struggles for men today? When the Jews exiled in Babylon learned that Cyrus had decreed their return, wise and experienced men knew that three challenges confronted yesterday's slaves: the difficulties of the painful journey across the desert to Jerusalem, the inevitable moments of failure that would punctuate their efforts, and the problem of an impoverished people rebuilding the temple that Solomon had raised in the golden age of Israel when, as the book of Kings records, "silver was as plentiful as stone in Jerusalem" (3 Kgs. 10:27). That these challenges were met and successfully answered contains lessons on another plane for those who are the spiritual descendants of the rebuilders of the earthly Jerusalem.

THE PARABLE OF A PILGRIM

If the warning of the *Imitation of Christ*, "not to dispute concerning the merits of the saints, as to who is more holy than another, or greater in the kingdom of heaven," must also be applied to books, then care should have been taken in the use of superlatives when speaking in times past of the seventeenth century English Benedictine's book, *Holy Wisdom* or *Sancta Sophia*. This treatise on contemplation was written by Father Augustine Baker who taught men that "To pray is not to talk, or think, but love" and so great was the esteem in which his work was once held that it was claimed (with pious hyperbole) that:

"England may now her *Saint-Sophia* boast:
A fairer too, than that the Grecians lost."

Father Baker borrows "The Parable of a Pilgrim" from an earlier author when he wants to illustrate "the necessity of a strong resolution and courage to persevere" in all those who set out to reach the heavenly Jerusalem of true peace and perfect union with God. From this parable we learn that only those reach their destination who, like the Jews returning from Babylon, mistrust their own strength and place all their trust in God. Here is the parable:

Once there was a man that had a great desire to go to Jerusalem; and because he knew not the right way, he addressed himself for advice to one that he hoped was not unskilfull in it, and asked whether there was any way passable thither. The other answered that the way thither was both long and full of very great difficulties; yea, that there were many ways that seemed and promised to lead thither, but the dangers of them were too great. Nevertheless, one way he knew which, if the pilgrim would diligently pursue according to the directions and marks that he would give him, — though said he, I cannot promise thee a security from many frights, beatings and other ill-usage and temptations of all kinds, but if thou canst have courage and patience enough to suffer them without quarreling, or resisting, or troubling thyself, and so pass on, having this only in thy mind, and sometimes on thy tongue, *I have nought, I am nought, I desire nought but to be at Jerusalem,* — then my life for thine, thou wilt escape safe with thy life and in a competent time arrive thither.

The pilgrim, it is hoped, followed this advice and reached Jerusalem as did the Jews who left the valleys of the Tigris and the Euphrates for the Valley of the Jordan. So shall all travelers arrive safely who leave this "valley of tears" and set out for the true Jerusalem, if in their hearts and on their lips be always the words: *"I am nought, I can do nought, I have nought, and nought do I desire to have, but only Jesus and His love."*

With the humility, charity and singleness of purpose that these words express, we too, in God's good time, will possess Jesus and His love.

PURIFICATION NOT GRATIFICATION

But the journey to Jerusalem was not the only challenge that the Jews faced and answered. Once they reached the holy city, new difficulties were in store. Work hard they did and over a long period but it was inevitable, as sooner or later it is inevitable in the life of every Christian, that they were convinced that they had failed. Days pass and years pass. We have not shirked our task yet the sickening realization forces itself upon us that we have accomplished very little; what is even harder to accept is the paralyzing fear that the days or years to come will be equally barren and bleak.

Judging from the space devoted to this subject in spiritual books, discouragement must be endemic in the lives of many who are engaged in building the City of God. This discouragement is due, in many instances, to a misunderstanding of the meaning of the word *success*.

The Jews who dreamed of building an Israel surpassing the earthly glory enjoyed by the united Kingdom ruled by David and Solomon set themselves a chimerical goal. Jacques Maritain warns us in *The Range of Reason* that those who struggle to win such success are doomed to fail. Then, as now, if a new and better age is to be inaugurated, secular life must be sanctified by spiritual experience, contemplative energies, brotherly love. Nor even when we make this our goal, as did many in Israel under the guidance of Esdras and Nehemias, can we be assured of seeing the results of our endeavors. Pascal's chiding words apply to men of every age: "We always behave as if we were called upon to make truth triumph, whereas we are called upon only to struggle for it."

Edward Leen, C.S.Sp., develops this idea in his book, *The Likeness of Christ*. We must take up our cross daily, he says, that is, face with courage the tasks that each day brings, intent only on doing them rightly and well, striving to succeed but not making success the condition of our efforts, acting because it is God's will and not because there is an opportunity of ministering to our egoism — it is only on these conditions that life will produce its transforming effect on us, and make us like Jesus, who "having joy set before Him, endured the cross, despising the shame."

We must not rebel against the plan of divine providence or frustrate this plan by our anger, despair, irritation or cowardice. The work we do does not matter but the effect of our work on us matters much. Purification, however painful, not gratification, however legitimate, is what life is meant to give. If we allow God to fashion us through the times, places, circumstances and companions that He has chosen for us in His love, then our lives will have something of the sublimity, nobility and true success of the life of Jesus. We may know failure but failure such as this is a triumph and as Father Leen concludes: "our passage through this world will become in a mysterious way a most potent influence in the diffusion of God's Kingdom on earth, and in the extension of the reign of Jesus Christ in the souls of men."

CENTRIPETAL AND CENTRIFUGAL LOVE

A third challenge for the Jews was rebuilding the temple. Their determination to rebuild the temple showed how important to them was this sign of Yahweh's abiding presence in their midst. The second temple, like the first, was one day to be destroyed but its meaning has never disappeared from the world; in fact its deepest significance was only to be disclosed with the coming of Jesus Christ and would be fully realized only in His Church.

A rich synthesis of the temple theme in the Mosaic traditions and the Gospel traditions has been brilliantly made by Father David Stanley, S.J. When God led the Israelites out of Egypt, He promised them that they would build Him a sanctuary and that He would dwell in it in their midst. About this sanctuary revolved their sacrificial cult. From it they learned that there is but one God and that He is all-holy. St. John shows the central position that the temple occupied in the life and teaching of Jesus. To those who demanded a "sign" in proof of His claims, He offered the "sign" of the temple: "Destroy this temple and in three days I will raise it up" (2:19). In the first part of the sentence, He alluded to the stone structure before Him, in the second to the temple of His glorified body which would be raised up, three days after His death. This new temple of which He spoke was His own glorified body which, like the ancient temple of Israel, was the dwelling place of God's "glory" and the symbol of God's abiding presence among men. It is in the Eucharist that all the various lines of the temple theme of the Old Testament and the New converge. The sacrament of His sacred Body should be the center of our lives: the heart of each life should be the Tabernacle with its centripetal and centrifugal Love.

The journey from the pagan world of Babylon was a long one, the struggle against discouragement was not always successful, the temple disappointed the men who remembered the splendors of the buildings the Babylonians had pillaged and leveled to the ground. Is this to say that the Chronicler's history concludes on a sorrowful note? Far from it. He set himself a higher aim and those who read his books come to the end convinced, as we shall be some day when we shall see our lives as God sees them, that His divine plan is beautiful, His worship is the most important act of our lives and His promises are never broken. Nor need we wait until we die to see all this. Faith can show it to us now — if we truly believe.

THE BOOK OF TOBIAS

THE LIFE of Tobias may be summed up in three phrases: loyal service, heart-breaking sorrows, blessed rewards. This devout Galilean refused to kneel before the golden calves Solomon's schismatic successor had set up when he reigned over the rebel tribes of the Northern Kingdom. Shunning the idolatry of the men of Nephthali, he went down at the appointed times to adore the true God in the temple at Jerusalem, bearing with him tithes and first-fruit offerings for himself and for the needs of the homeless poor. He chose a wife from his own tribe and they gave their only child, a son much like his father, the same beautiful name which is at once a profession of faith, an act of love, a prayer of trust: because Tobias is an abbreviation of the Hebrew *Tobiahu* which means "God is good."

A TEST OF LOVE

When the Assyrians overran Israel in 721 B.C. and carried the Jews into captivity, Tobias, Anna and the young Tobias began the suffering life of exiles in a strange land. In Rages, later in Nineveh, as once in Galilee, Tobias was faithful in his observance of the Law and fearless in the service of his neighbor. It was his "daily task to visit his own clansmen, comforting them and providing for each of them as best he could, out of what store he had; it was for him to feed the hungry, to clothe the naked, to honor with careful burial men that had died of sickness and men slain" (1:19f.).

God's ways are sometimes strange. In a quick succession of disasters this faithful servant was deprived of honor, riches and health. Disgrace, poverty and blindness came to test his love. With true nobility of soul his answer was one of thanksgiving — thanksgiving to God, the author and giver of life.

Family and friends taunted him, asking of what use had been his years of obedience, his almsgiving and all his acts of merciful love. Stoutly he resisted them with words like these: "Never talk like this; we come of holy stock, you and I; and God has life waiting for us if we will keep faith with Him" (2:17). Still another trial awaited him, because the soul who meets outward misfortune and the mocking words of men must undergo a third and far more subtle testing.

That trouble should afflict us and men fail us is not surprising but that God should seem indifferent to our pleading is an agony hard to bear. Gerard Manley Hopkins knew a similar struggle and he could write:

O the mind, mind has mountains; cliffs of fall

Frightful, sheer, no-man-fathomed. Hold them cheap

May who ne'er hung there.

In darkness Tobias prayed and his final act of surrender is the strengthening one that we find again in the New Testament and that we may well want to make our own: "O Lord, do with me according to Your will."

Death for which he prayed was not part of God's plan. New griefs were in store. Years earlier when he had been rich and the king's friend, he had loaned a kinsman a large sum of money. Although his debtor lived far from Nineveh, although the journey was full of dangers, although his only son was young and inexperienced, Tobias decided to send the boy to recover the money.

A guide was found who said he knew the way and claimed, moreover, to be acquainted with Gabelus to whom Tobias had given the ten silver talents long ago. Sadly he and his wife kissed the boy. With tears and good advice they bade him goodbye and prayed for him as he started off with his kindly guide and frisky little dog.

Weeks passed. Fears which at first seemed groundless now seemed prophetic. No longer able to comfort his wife, Tobias could only ask himself: "What means this long delay? What has detained the boy?" Anna was restless in her grief. She went into the city. She watched the roads. She questioned every traveler. But to her patient husband sitting with closed eyes at home she could bring no quieting hope. To wait is a form of service God sometimes asks of those He loves.

ALL THINGS

At last there is a sudden shift of tone and the story comes to a happy ending: the long-awaited traveler returns, bringing with him a cure for his father's blindness, treasure enough to restore the family fortunes, and a bride whom God has visibly blessed. The trusted guide reveals himself to be Raphael, an archangel, "one of the seven who minister before the throne of God." Then he returns to heaven while his startled benefactors watch him vanish from their sight.

There is general rejoicing, and as we close the book the words St. Paul wrote to the Romans are ringing in our ears with all the triumph of a final, satisfying chord: "We know that to them that love God all things work together unto good" (Rom. 8:28).

LITERARY FORM

Present day widespread and growing interest in the Bible was heralded and made possible by the Encyclical *Divino afflante Spiritu* of 1943 in which Pope Pius XII urged scholars "to unlock the treasures of God's word" so that all may know "how good and sweet is the Spirit of the Lord." One of the "keys" the Holy Father recommends is the study of literary forms which will open to us the divinely inspired "literal sense" of the sacred books. He says:

> In many cases in which the sacred authors are accused of some historical inaccuracy or of the inexact recording of some events, it is found to be a question of nothing more than those customary and characteristic forms of expression or styles of narrative which were current in human communication among the ancients, and which were in fact quite commonly and legitimately employed.

This principle helps us to understand many things about the book of Tobias. The Church has always included it among the inspired books but has made no definite pronouncement concerning its literary form. Many scholars teach that the author has given his story a true historical setting but that his principal purpose is didactic. It is often difficult to distinguish between the historical nucleus and the author's own contribution.

Who is the author? When and where did he compose this book? The imperfect condition of the oldest texts makes these questions hard to answer. It would seem that he lived during the third century, wrote in Palestine or Egypt, was a gifted man and deeply religious.

OUR TIMES ARE IN HIS HAND

Into his narrative he has woven certain well established facts and he has given his edifying story unity of focus, cleverly contrived complications and characters made living through dialogue and action. Some of the incidents have been compared with the adventures of a perennially favorite folklore hero whom the Egyptians called Ahikar.

But more significant are the beautiful allusions to the book of Genesis; we are reminded of the marriages of Rebecca and Rachel; we find interesting parallels with the life of Joseph; certain scenes remind us of Ruth; and the author himself speaks of the resemblance of Tobias with Job. As in the use of our Lord's parables the value of this book is to be found not in its historical facts but in a great truth simply told:

> Our times are in His hand
> Who saith "A whole I planned,
> Youth shows but half; trust God, see all, nor be afraid!"

Tobias is not to be found in Jewish and Protestant Bibles, but its position in the Catholic canon is recognized by the early Fathers and councils. Few books have been used so widely in the liturgy. More than 100 of its 298 verses are found in the official prayer of the Church.

GIVING JOY . . . RECEIVE GLADNESS

They appear in the second nocturns of the third week of September, personalizing, as in the readings from Job which precede, and from Judith and Esther which will follow at the end of the month, ideals of patient suffering and courageous love which were presented in speculative form in the August breviary lessons taken from the books of Wisdom. The patristic comment shows us what the Church considers to be one of the important lessons of Tobias: the social value of fasting and almsgiving. Pope St. Leo in his embertide sermon says:

> We need to be cleansed from the stain of our sin by fasting and almsgiving. . . . Beloved, let us hunger a little and take away some small portion from our habitual measure in order that we may help the poor . . . While you are giving joy [by your liberality] you will receive gladness.

BLESS THE GOD OF HEAVEN

The responsory to this wholesome advice is taken from the twelfth chapter of Tobias in which the boy asks his father how he can repay his wonder-working guide:

He it was that escorted me safely, going and coming; recovered the debt from Gabelus, won me my bride; rid her of the fiend's attack; engaged the gratitude of her parents; rescued me from the fish's onslaught; and to thee restored the light of day. Through him we have been loaded with benefits; is it possible to make any return for all these? (12:3).

They then offer him half their new-found wealth and the angel (whom they yet do not know) bids them instead give thanks to God. His words form the responsory that is repeated every day during the third week:

> Blessed be the God of heaven,
> Give glory to Him in the sight of all that live,
> Because He has shown His mercy to you (12:6).

This same text is found in several different forms in the missal, so that we cannot help asking ourselves what rules (if any) govern the liturgical use of Scripture.

The answer is instructive. Scholars like Fr. William Heidt, O.S.B., explain that in the liturgy, as in all prayer, there is a double movement: we speak to God and God speaks to us. In those parts of the liturgy where God speaks to us (in the breviary lessons, in the epistles and gospels of the Mass) we may not alter God's words, we may not add to nor subtract from their divinely inspired meaning. Experts speaking to experts would put it this way: "Here principles of hermeneutics taught in General Introduction must be strictly observed."

Greater freedom but the same reverence governs the use the Church makes of God's words in those parts of the liturgy where we speak to God (the responsories of the breviary, the parts of the Mass sung by the choir, etc.). Here the words may be considered apart from the meaning that is theirs in their biblical setting. They are meant to be the expression of our shame, our hunger, our wondering awe as we celebrate the day's feast or repeat some definitely orientated liturgical formula. They can give a new dimension to our petitions or to our thanksgiving. They can make our material needs or the heart's deep-hidden hope part of the great prayer of the whole body of which Christ is the head. To express it technically: "In a devotional context accommodation by extension and by allusion is legitimate if it be dogmatically sound."

In the light of these remarks it is interesting to consider the application of the responsory cited above. On Sunday of the third week in September it follows St. Leo's plea for fasting, and the words "blessed

be God . . ." become our prayer of thanksgiving for the benefits St.
Leo tells us that our fasting will bring to our neighbor and to ourselves.
On Monday the responsory follows the story of Tobias' blindness and
it expresses our gratitude for the shining examples of patience He has
given us in His servants Tobias and Job. On Tuesday it follows Tobias'
humble acceptance of his wife's bitter outburst and it is the continuation
of his affirmation that all God's words are justice, mercy and truth.
On Wednesday it is a statement of our faith in answer to our Lord's rebuke to an incredulous generation. On Thursday it continues Raphael's
admonition to Tobias and his son. On Friday it follows the story of
Christ's kindness to a sinful woman and it becomes our acknowledgment that we, too, have received mercy from Him. On Saturday it is a
paean of praise because God, according to the homily of St. Gregory,
has lovingly sought the human race "before the law, under the law and
under grace."

BLESSED BE THE HOLY TRINITY

The same Scripture text is used in the Mass for Trinity Sunday. Three
times when we speak to God (in the introit, the offertory and the communion), the Church places on our lips the angel's words with appropriate allusions to the feast. The reverent melody of the chant for the
introit is a worthy setting for our tribute of adoring love:

> Blessed be the holy Trinity and undivided Unity,
> To Him we give glory
> Because He has shown us His mercy.

Another adaptation of the same text is found in the offertory. Here
each of the three divine Persons is named. We bless them because
we have just been told in the gospel that it is in their name that the
apostles went forth to preach and to release through the sacraments
torrents of compassionate love:

> Blessed be God the Father
> And His only-begotten Son and the Holy Spirit,
> Because He has shown us His mercy.

In the communion antiphon the words of the angel are repeated once
again, here the verbs alone are changed. United to Christ in the sacrament of divine pity we sing our hymn of praise:

> Let us bless the God of heaven
> And praise Him before all who live,
> Because He has shown us His mercy.

JOY BE TO THEE ALWAYS!

A similar study might be made of the seven uses of the first responsory for the third week of September: "Lord, do not remember my sins, or those of our fathers, nor punish us for our misdeeds" (3:3). These words are also found in several other contexts: in the priest's preparation before Mass, in the rite of exorcism, in the blessing of an abbot, and in the blessing given the soul at the hour of death. The felicitous application of the text in each of these cases is obvious.

So beautiful a picture of the love of father, mother and child is given in the book of Tobias, that it is appropriate that the introit for the nuptial Mass be taken from its pages (7:15; 8:19). Curiously the reformers of sixteenth century Germany, who refused to place this book in their Bibles, encouraged their people to attend the popular "Tobias Dramas," which tell the story of his life and extol the virtues of married love.

Dr. John Hennig, to whom all who study the relation of Scripture and liturgy are indebted for his painstaking research, points out that almost all the Scripture for the feast of St. Raphael on October 24 is taken from the book of Tobias. The epistle gives us the well-known words of the angel: "It is good to hide the secret of a king: but honorable to reveal and confess the works of God" (12:7–15), and the alleluia verse contains his gracious greeting: "Joy be to thee always!" (5:11). In the Raccolta there is an indulgenced prayer for emigrants which tells the story of the angel's visit to Tobias and concludes with the petition that he will give us like protection. In the Mozarabic Liber he is invoked in the blessing of incense. By Pseudo-Cyprian he is called "the angel of penance" and he is asked to free us from our sins as he once freed the bride of the young Tobias from the evil spirit.

MAY HE REIGN FOREVER AS OUR KING

Tobias has fourteen chapters. It is one of the shorter books of the Bible. St. Jerome tells us that he was able to translate it in a single day with the help of a hired interpreter who knew Chaldean and Hebrew. "What he said to me in Hebrew that I rendered into Latin to a notary whom I had engaged." While we must admire the Saint's zeal and we like to think of the good use he would have made of a dictaphone and other modern speed devices, we cannot help thinking that had he used some slower method he might have given us a smoother Latin version.

But nothing can detract from the beauty of its teaching. Let us see what the author can tell us about God. (For the convenience of those who would like to make a more thorough study of the passages, chapter and verse are given).

Praise befits the Lord whose name is great forever, of whose kingdom there will be no end (13:1–4). All-wise are His designs, their meaning hidden from our eyes (3:19), their power knows no measure but the measurelessness of His love (7:14). The trials He sends prove the soul's true worth (12:13), His punishments are gateways for His mercy (3:22). The just soul finds content in Him (13:10), the sinner pardon (13:6), the sick relief (11:15), the poor redress (9:7); none can escape His hand (13:2). Nations from afar shall come to Him and shall bring gifts (13:14). His sons shall worship Him for He is their Lord and God (13:4). His angels stand before Him (12:15), with prayers and praise they speak to Him of men (12:12). He has delivered Jerusalem (13:19); with ophir-gold its streets are paved (13:22). Blessed be the Lord! He is good! May he reign forever as our king! (13:23).

HOLY FADER . . . SAYNT TOBY

Few full commentaries were written on Tobias by the Fathers. St. Ambrose devoted twenty-four chapters to the book; three of the chapters give a summary of its contents, the other twenty-one are a warning against usury. Bede wrote what he called "an allegorical interpretation," Strabo and many others followed Bede's example.

Still medieval Christians loved Tobias. The Stowe Missal does not hesitate to call him a saint. The Sarum Breviary lists his feast for September 11. The 1526 *Martirologe in Englysshe* has this entry for September 14: "The feest also of the holy fader of the olde testament saynt Toby. And of the famous wydowe saynt Iudith . . . and of saynt Hester."

How well, we wonder, as we read the story of Tobias, would the sanctity here portrayed measure up to the strict requirements for heroic virtue laid down by the wisely exacting canonist Benedict XIV? And what is the one lesson that gives the key to all that good "Saynt Toby" did?

The Pope says that four things are required for proven or manifest heroic virtue: (1) the matter or object should be difficult, beyond the common strength of man; (2) the acts should be performed promptly and easily; (3) they should be accomplished with holy joy; (4) they should be made frequently, whenever an opportunity to perform them presents itself.

Heroic, indeed, seems to be the measure of the virtue portrayed for us in this book. And the key to all teachings seems to be unfailing trust in divine Providence. This is taught on every page.

UNFAILING TRUST

St. Thomas explains that Providence in God corresponds to the virtue of prudence in us: it is the wise regulation of means to attain an end. Now the purpose of all things, big and little, is to manifest God's goodness. To the infinite wisdom and goodness of Providence we must unconditionally surrender ourselves because everything that happens has been willed by God or has been permitted by Him and He wills nothing but for our good and for His glory. Therefore we must conform ourselves to the divine will as it is manifestly expressed and we must abandon ourselves to the divine will of His good pleasure, crucifying though it may be.

Constantly submitting to God's action in our lives, welcoming the joy or the pain He sends, striving faithfully to keep His law, we will "serve the Lord in truth and seek to do the things that please Him." Then we will find that, like Tobias, the rest of our days "will be in joy, in peace and in the fear of the Lord."

THE BOOK OF JUDITH

BY WHAT right, sirs, do you put the Lord's goodness to such a test? Would you set a date to the Lord's mercies, bid Him keep tryst with you on a day of your own appointing?" The elders were silent. In measured words Judith laid down a more suitable procedure, one assured, so she declared, of success. "Abate we our pride, and wait on Him with chastened spirits; entreat Him with tears to grant us relief at a time of His own choosing. He, the Lord our God, will bring the invader low, and disappoint him of his prize."

To Judith's just rebuke the elders of Bethulia could offer no reply; to her insistence on humble prayer, penance and an unconditioned trust they could only agree. While the woman's serene courage wins our admiration, the men's fears seem to be only too well founded.

They were realists. They knew that their city's plight was past all human aid. Besieging Assyrians "swarmed like locusts" outside the well-built city walls. A long baggage-train and an endless array of camels provided for the army's many needs. Fresh supplies were arriving from conquered foes. Corn they had in abundance. There were oxen, too, and sheep past all counting. In addition Holofernes, Nabuchodonosor's boldest commander, had "a great store of gold and silver from the royal treasury."

Yet, more potent than all these resources was the king's express desire that the whole world be brought under his allegiance. The conquest must be total. Holofernes had been warned that nowhere was pity to melt his soldier's heart, no fortified town was to resist his dominion.

WITHIN FIVE DAYS

And resisting his dominion was just what the men of Bethulia had done. All other nations had surrendered, defeated either by the monarch's mighty forces or by their own fears. Their lands were devastated, their sanctuaries leveled to the ground. Unwilling that the temple suffer a similar fate, Eliachim, the high priest, asked that the invading forces be resisted as they poured through the passes in the hill country of Ephraim north of Jerusalem. Day and night the men of Bethulia obeyed. Only a narrow pass led between the mountains, this they controlled. Here a handful of men could hold a host at bay.

Holofernes was not to be outwitted. Scouts must find for him a devious path so that these mountain-folk might be circumvented and come to feel the cold Assyrian sword. But the scouts brought back a better plan. "Force no battle. Make no attack by stealth," they said. "Instead cut off the aqueduct that brings these people water. Set a guard around some springs that are near the city walls. Either you will compass their deaths, and no blood shed, or, worn down at last they will yield into your hands the city they think impregnable."

Twenty days passed. Undone by thirst, weakened by hunger, husbands and wives, young men and children cried out that a swift death at the sword's point was better than a lingering death from parching thirst. Ozias the Simeonite, the elder who had first counseled resistance, could only answer: "Brethren, be calm and patient. These five next days, let us still look to the Lord for deliverance; perhaps His anger will relent, perhaps He means to win himself fresh renown. If at the end of those five days no help has reached you, rest assured we will act on the counsel you have given."

A FAIR AND FERVENT WIDOW

It was this decision to surrender the city that Judith so condemned. Summoning two of the elders, the fair and fervent widow exhorted them to pray, to inspire the people with courage and to believe that God, through her, would bring His people peace.

That night Judith, accompanied by her maid, left the city. For three years she had been a widow. Her husband had died in early spring when the barley was being harvested. She was breath-takingly beautiful and she had great wealth, a full household, and lands well-stocked with cattle

and sheep. Men everywhere held her in high repute. They knew her to
be the Lord's devout worshiper. No one could find a word to say in her
dispraise.

Now she laid aside her sackcloth, folded her widow's robes, donned
the garments of her happier days and taking jeweled bracelets and
anklets, earrings and finger-rings, hastened to the city gate. All who
saw her marveled at her beauty. Asking no questions, they let her pass.
"May the God of our fathers," the elders said, "grant you His favor,
and His strength speed whatever design is in your heart." And all who
watched cried out "Amen." So with a prayer she left the city.

Making her way down the mountain-slope she came at break of day
to the surprised Assyrian sentinel. And while he marveled at her beauty
she told him of her desire to gain audience with Holofernes, so that she
might acquaint him with the weakness of Bethulia and show him how
to capture the city without the loss of a single man.

For so charming a deserter with so attractive a plan access to the
commander's tent could be arranged at once. "No sooner did she stand
before him than Holofernes' eyes made him her prisoner." He applauded
her escape from a city she predicted would soon be his prize because
her people must in their hunger offend their God by taking forbidden
food. He praised her plan of waiting at his side until she learned in
prayer that the Israelites had, by their transgression, forfeited divine
help and could swiftly be subdued.

YOUR NAME SHALL BE FOREVER BLESSED

And so the story draws to its triumphant close. For the next three nights
Judith was allowed to live according to the prescriptions Moses had
given his people long ago. Each day before dawn she left the tent
Holofernes had set apart for her use and she went out of the camp into
the vale of Bethulia with her maid to pray that God would speed her
task. On the fourth night she attended a banquet at which Holofernes,
drowsy with wine, could offer no resistance when she raised his own
scimitar against him. Before dawn she left the tent as usual, her handmaid bearing in her wallet Holofernes' severed head.

No conqueror could receive more glorious a welcome than awaited
the fearless widow when she entered the city she had left so near defeat
four days before. No commander could have been obeyed with more
alacrity than was Judith when she ordered: "Hang this trophy from the
battlements. At sunrise feign attack. The Assyrians on learning that

their leader is dead will be ready for flight. Go after them undismayed, the Lord will give you victory."

When the elders in Jerusalem learned of the enemy's routing, Eliachim led them to Bethulia. There they extolled Judith in the presence of all the people, saying: "You are the boast of Jerusalem, the joy of Israel, the pride of our people; you have played a man's part and kept your courage high. Not unrewarded is your love of chastity . . . the Lord gave you firmness of resolve, and your name shall be ever blessed."

And to all the elders said, the people answered Amen.

IN WONDERMENT OF HER BEAUTY

The author of this stirring tale is unknown. Internal evidence suggests that he was a Palestinian Jew who lived in the first or second century before Christ. He probably wrote in Hebrew and he undoubtedly wrote with artistry and skill. Two examples may be alleged in support of this claim.

Many critics noting Gotthold Lessing's observation claim that this unknown writer deserves to be compared with Homer. In his study of the limits of painting and poetry Lessing points out that nowhere does Homer enter upon a detailed description of Helen of Troy, yet her beauty is the basis for the whole of the Iliad. A lesser poet would have ventured upon such a description but Homer knew how to convey an idea of Helen's beauty which "far exceeds anything that art with this aim is able to accomplish."

We have only to recall the passage where Helen draws near an assembly of elders near the Skaian gate. The venerable old men see her and confess: "Small blame is it that Trojans and well-greaved Achaians should for such a woman long time suffer hardships." What the poet does not describe in each separate part, he forces us to acknowledge in its effects. The old men's admiration gives us a higher sense of surpassing personal beauty than could have been conveyed with many words.

So, too, with Judith. The author gives no description of her beauty, but that it was very great we are forced to acknowledge. We observe that when the elders of Bethulia saw her reach the city gate, "they fell into great wonderment of her beauty," and they begged God to prosper her errand with these words: "Cause may Jerusalem have to be proud of you; may your name live among the holy and just."

The second example of the author's technical competence may be found in his handling of subsidiary themes. The most notable is that of the inclusion in God's salvific plan of hated enemies of the Jews. In this respect the sub-plot dealing with Achior is profoundly significant. This Ammonite chieftain was fighting on the side of Holofernes. When the men of Bethulia resisted the Assyrians, Achior, instead of arousing the commander's wrath against the Israelites, sought to inspire in him a salutary fear of men so favored by God.

Each time he repeats his story, first to Holofernes, later to the Jews to whom Holofernes had surrendered him, Achior's faith in the one true God puts the Jews to shame and his message of loyal service has the majesty and force of the words of their own inspired prophets. Small wonder that his story has a happy ending. Casting paganism aside, he embraced the religion of the people he had helped to save and he declared that wherever Judith's tale is told the God of Israel shall be glorified.

BUT IS IT HISTORY?

Poetry, we know, may be of many genres: dramatic, narrative, epic and lyric. History, so Toynbee tells us, has availed itself of all of these. The lyrical form, he explains, has many facets. It may present itself in exultation over a liberation, in pride over an achievement, in praise of heroism. Surely the story of the freeing of Bethulia belongs with all stirring tales of victory heroically won against oppressors and in face of overwhelming odds. Lyrical in this sense, the book of Judith certainly is. But is it history?

No original text is extant. Words and sentence structure of the Greek version suggest that the story first was recorded in Hebrew. In one night St. Jerome, to please some friends, made a free Latin version of an Aramaic exemplar and this with all its puzzling problems is in the Vulgate today. The councils of Trent and Vatican, following an old tradition and the legislation of fourth century Roman and African synods, recognized its canonical status.

Its place among the sacred books is sure. But scholars ask whether it is history or fiction or a combination of both. Names of persons and places appear in strange combinations. Chronological patterns are perplexing. Persian and Greek allusions increase geographical incongruities. In all of these the author was obviously not interested. His record of an historical event, embellished as it may be, is meant to entertain as well as to instruct. In a carefully fashioned narrative he shows that God the Creator of the world is the triumphant Master of history. All-merciful and all-just He chastises His people's adversaries when His people call upon Him with penance, faith and prayer.

These lessons would be timely in any age but to men and women facing perils similar to those over which Judith so successfully triumphed they would have special meaning. To write like this would be to write history in a broad sense, making use of a definite historical foundation in order to give an example of heroic virtue and to show God's unfailing providence. Whatever conclusion scholars reach about the literary form, it is this profound purpose of the inspired writer that well deserves to be made the subject of our prayer.

PIETY AND PATRIOTISM . . . CHASTITY AND COURAGE

Judith, it is seen, takes her place among the great women of the Old Testament. Yet Jewish history contains no mention of her name. We are reminded of Jael, the intrepid Israelite of the north, who, in the days of the Judges, slew a national enemy single handed and whose praises Debbora sang (Jdgs.5). We are reminded, too, of Esther who set aside her humble garb and in queenly robes dazzled all beholders and won mercy for her people from a hostile Persian king (Est. 14).

But Judith, unlike Esther, has not found her Racine. Paul Claudel captured some of her nobility in his austere and involved verse and a five act tragedy by E. Le Minime is the most successful modern attempt to portray on the stage her piety and patriotism, her chastity and courage, virtues which are so travestied in the dramas of men like Arnold Bennett, Henry Bernstein and Jean Giraudoux.

Nor are the librettos flawless which were used by Mozart and Honegger, though the music they have written in her honor deserves to be better known. Mozart was only fifteen when he composed the oratorio *Betulia Liberata* with its superb choruses, brilliant arias, cleverly incorporated psalm-tones and well-knit themes. A more mature Mozart would have given us something warmer, more personal, more worthy of the heroine whom all Bethulia loved.

Arthur Honegger, the contemporary Swiss-French composer, found in her story a subject suited to his polytonal style. With incisive rhythms and keen dissonances his music ranges from biting satire to reverent prayer. He makes a brilliant contrast between the barbarian camp of the Assyrians with all its insolence, violence and arrogant pride, and the besieged city of Bethulia with all its suffering, grief and dread. Judith is another Joan of Arc in her sense of mission, her openness to God's good pleasure. She has the greatness of a national heroine and the simplicity of a happy child.

Some of these lovely qualities may be learned from some recommended passages:

Let us prove to the world that Nabuchodonosor rules it, and other God there is none . . . (5:1–7:25).

Now let us turn to one whom all this news concerned, a widow called Judith . . . (8:1–8:34).

Still from a humble soul, an obedient will, the prayer must come that wins you . . . (9:1–10:9).

Compose yourself, Holofernes said, no need your heart should misgive you . . . (10:10–12:12).

Open the gates! God is on our side! Open the gates! His power lives in Israel . . . (13:13–15:8).

You are the boast of Jerusalem, the joy of Israel, the pride of our people . . . (15:9–16:31).

WORTHY OF PRAISE OR BLAME

Trópos is a Greek word that means "a way of life." Exegetes sometimes ask in what moral or tropological sense certain passages of sacred Scripture are to be understood. What rules can such passages provide for right conduct? This question is at first disquieting when raised about some of Judith's words and deeds.

It would seem that she lied to the Assyrian guards and to Holofernes, that she used her personal charms to arouse his base passions, that she imprudently went to visit him, that with careful premeditation she encompassed his death. Lies, provocation to evil, grave moral imprudence, murder: is Judith to be praised or blamed?

In the Bible she is praised, the Fathers of the Church in commentaries and sermons hold her up for our admiration, spiritual writers draw many lessons from her conduct. A solution to this difficulty may be expressed this way:

From the subjective point of view she seems above reproach. She acted in good faith. Her motives were patriotic and religious. She had constant recourse to God in prayer. The highest officials of church and state, knowing all the details, warmly commended all she did without any reservations.

Today from an objective point of view our judgment might be more severe. The inspired writer recorded Judith's conduct but this does not necessarily imply his approval. Nor can we conclude that because she was praised for her heroic patriotism she was blameless in everything she did. St. Thomas frankly faces this fact. He says: "Judith is praised not for the lies she told Holofernes but because of her affection for the salvation of her people, for whose sake she exposed herself to danger."

In forming our final judgment we must also remember that these things took place in pre-Christian times among people whose customs and thought-patterns differ from our own, during a war against a cruel and deadly foe, and that all that Judith said and did was designed to bring about her country's good. Perhaps, we may add, she had received some inner assurance that God would protect her on a mission she had placed under His all-powerful care.

HOLINESS AND VALOR

Chivalry or charity or a combination of the two lead the Fathers to speak of her in glowing terms. Clement of Alexandria hails her as a perfect woman, lacking no needful virtue. Origen devotes a homily to her heroism and extols her magnificence and nobility. Ambrose declares that she is holy, worthy of admiration and highly to be praised for her fasting. Fulgentius speaks of her beauty and her intelligence, of her contempt for earthly vanities and of her love of heavenly virtue. St. Augustine cites her purity, her powerful prayer, her intrepid victory. Others commend her for her generosity in freeing her serving-maid or for her unselfishness in keeping for herself no part of the booty.

More recent writers draw some unexpected lessons. Let us quote two. Where moralists might pause to question Judith's concern about her personal adornment, St. Francis of Sales hastens to find a deeper meaning than vanity and a desire to please. He says:

> Judith always wore her weeds of mourning except when she assumed her costly festive robes and went forth by God's inspiration to overthrow Holofernes. So should it be with us, we should remain peacefully clad in our misery and abjection amid our imperfections and infirmities until God shall raise us to deeds of greater valor.

St. John of the Cross in reading Judith's rebuke to the elders who had agreed to pray for five days and then, no help coming, to surrender the city, fears that readers may conclude that novenas and such devotions are of little worth. He would have such persons know that God is well pleased with these devotions provided that "the rejoicing and strength of the will" are directed to Him alone. The saint continues:

> I do not for this reason condemn — nay, I rather approve — the fixing of days on which certain persons sometimes arrange to make their devotions, such as novenas, or other such things. I condemn only their conduct as

concerns the fixity of their methods and the ceremonies with which they practise them. Even so did Judith rebuke and reprove the people of Bethulia because they had limited God as to the time wherein they hoped for His mercy, saying: "Do ye set God a time for His mercies?" This, she says, is not to move God to clemency, but to awaken His wrath.

EVERY HATRED IS CAUSED BY LOVE

Many great masters have made Judith the subject of their art and almost all their pictures fail to satisfy. In the Uffici, Botticelli's Judith shows the energy of a great emotion but her swiftly moving figure is all light and grace and lacks the fixity of firm resolve. Allori, in the Pitti, makes her a well-built, handsome woman but without the spiritual beauty that must have been hers in an abundant measure. Paul Veronese represents an exquisite young Venetian more likely to be interested in her magnificent pearls than in her country's fate. Tintoretto shows Judith at the gruesome moment of Holofernes' death — an unpleasant portrayal from which we quickly turn away.

For all their genius these men have failed to grasp why souls eager to serve God more valiantly turn to thoughts of Judith in their prayer. St. Thomas Aquinas has expressed this quality in a single sentence. "Every hatred is caused by love." He explains that love always precedes and "nothing is hated, save through being contrary to something dearly loved." So great was Judith's love for God and for His people that she could hate with a great hatred all that was opposed to Him and to those He loves. So great was her love (and consequently her hatred) that she was willing to act as His instrument in crushing evil as personified in the enemy seeking to destroy God's chosen people.

This truth is recognized in the liturgy when the great warrior maiden of France, Joan of Arc, is honored on her feast with several quotations from the book of Judith. Joan's great deeds of love and hatred deserve to be praised with these words of the alleluia verse: "You have played a man's part and kept your courage high: the Lord gave you firmness of resolve and your name shall be forever blessed. Pray for us, holy woman that you are, and the Lord's true worshiper" (Jud. 15:11; 8; 29; cf. also Jud. 5:8–11; 13:17f.).

YOUR PRAISE SHALL NEVER DIE

This close relation between our love for God and our hatred for all that is opposed to God explains why our Lady has been extolled in the gradual of the feast of the Immaculate Conception with words taken from the book of Judith: "Blessing be yours, Virgin Mary, from the Lord God the most high, such as no other woman on earth can claim.

You are the boast of Jerusalem, the joy of Israel, the glory of our people" (13:23; 15:10).

A similar combination of texts appears in the lesson of the new Mass of the Assumption (13:22–25; 15:10) and gives liturgical emphasis to the connection between the two mysteries. As the Holy Father says in the brief commentary on the definition of the dogma of the Assumption in the Apostolic Constitution *Munificentissimus Deus*, many had seen in the dogma of the preservation of Mary from all sin the root reasons for the incorruptibility of her body and her eventual assumption, body and soul, into the glories of heaven. Of Mary, as of Judith before her, it can truly be said: "Blessed be the Lord, maker of heaven and earth, for sending you to wound the head of our archenemy. Such high renown He has given you this day, that your praise shall never die. . . ."

Verses from the book of Judith are found in the Masses for the feasts of St. Lawrence of Brindisi and St. John Capistran and emphasize the historical connection between these heroic leaders. Another interesting use of this book occurs in the collect in time of war. But it is most often to honor our Lady that the Church makes liturgical reference to the protector of Bethulia, expressing in this way the belief that Mary in her beauty and in her love for her people will be forever their sure defence. Is she not hailed as one who is as glorious as the sun, as fair as the moon, and as awe-inspiring as an army set in battle array?

TO TRUST ONLY IN HIM

One final question must be considered. As we close the book of Judith what is the single quality that marks her so distinctively as a great soul? This quality seems to be her perfect serenity. Aware of the immense dangers that confronted her people and conscious of the obstacles to be overcome, she deliberately faced all perils and calmly went ahead. That, too, can be our attitude to life, if like Judith, we are strong enough to hope in God when there seems no reason still to hope.

Søren Kierkegaard writes: To be "in danger above seventy fathoms of water, many miles from all help, there to be joyful — that is great."

Of this greatness Judith was capable because she had a deep sense of the will of God and she realized that all things come from Him and are meant to bring us closer to Him. Her serenity comes only to those who love, to those who through love seek only the pleasure of the beloved, to those who with their whole hearts can repeat Judith's prayer: "God of the heavens, Maker of the floods, Lord of this universal frame, listen to the defenseless plea of one who trusts only in Your mercy." Prayer like this is always heard.

THE BOOK OF ESTHER

ESTHER was a brave, beautiful, devout Jewess who lived in the Persian capital of Susa during the Babylonian exile. Her mother and father were dead. Her foster-father Mardochai, of the tribe of Benjamin, was a man of strong religious convictions who carefully raised the little girl to know and love God. He was a true friend to his own people, captives like himself in a strange land. When the story opens, he is troubled.

In a dream he had seen a great disturbance over the earth. There were voices and tumults, thunders and earthquakes. Two mighty dragons confronted one another. All nations rose to fight against the nation of the just. In that day of darkness and danger, he watched a little fountain grow into a great river, darkness gave way to light, the sun moved majestically across the heavens, the humble were exalted and the mighty ones of this earth were destroyed.

Mardochai did not know what this meant because for him there were no secondary causes, divine Providence governed all things. So his trouble was replaced by trust and he waited to see "what God would do" (11:5–12).

Events followed fast. King Xerxes (or Assuerus) held a great banquet. During the celebration Queen Vasthi was deposed. Search was made throughout Persia for her successor. Esther was crowned. Who she was or from what people she came, no one asked. Her graciousness, her modesty, her regal dignity assured her a position of importance at

138

court. Yet the king's memory was short. Soon he seemed to have forgotten her. Other favorites captured his attention. Esther remained in
the palace, but was no longer summoned into the royal presence. To
enter that presence without a summons meant instant death.

God willed that at this time she render the king a signal service. Mardochai told her of a plot against the king's life. Esther made this known.
The king was saved and court historians promptly made an entry in the
royal annals of Mardochai's loyal deed.

Then Mardochai discovered a second conspiracy. Aman, his bitter
foe, the most powerful man at court, had ordered, with the king's approval, a massacre of all the Jews. Mardochai prayed, clothed in sackcloth and ashes. He sent a trusted messenger to Esther asking her to go
to the king and intercede for her people. To do this, he knew, might
mean her death, but he told her that her intercession alone could save
the Jews and that God, perhaps, had placed her at court for this great
act of clemency. Esther answered:

Go, and gather together all the Jews
whom you shall find in Susa, and pray ye for me. Neither eat nor drink for
three days and three nights; and I with my handmaids will fast in like
manner, and then I will go into the king, against the law, not being called,
and expose myself to death and to danger (4:16).

On the third day, despite her fear, she went to the king. Seeing her,
he was pleased: "What do you want, Queen Esther? What is your request? If you should ask for even one half of the kingdom, it shall be
given you."

And so the story has a happy ending. Mardochai received the honors
Aman had hoped would be given to himself. The Jews were allowed to
defend themselves against their foes. Esther's power of intercession was
vindicated before all nations.

The meaning of Mardochai's dream is now clear. He explained it in
these words:

God has done these things. I remember a dream that I saw,
which signified these same things; and nothing thereof has failed. The little
fountain which grew into a river, and was turned into a light, and into the
sun, and abounded into many waters, is Esther, whom the king married, and
made queen. But the two dragons are I and Aman. . . . And my nation is
Israel, who cried to the Lord, and the Lord saved His people; and He delivered us from all evils, and has wrought great signs and wonders among
the nations. He has remembered His people and has had mercy on His inheritance (cf. 10:1–12).

A DAY OF FEASTING, JOY AND BANQUETS

There are two ancient texts of the book of Esther. The Hebrew text is shorter and omits some passages that are found in the Greek text. St. Jerome made a literal translation of the Hebrew text. This we find in chapters 1–10:3 of our Bibles which are based on the Vulgate. He then made a free translation of the passages found only in the Greek text and placed them at the end of the book, chapters 10:4–16:24. The Council of Trent solemnly defined the canonicity of Esther, including the passages from the Greek.

Scholars find in this book an interesting question of literary form. Is it a true history? Or is it pure fiction? Or is it history treated creatively by an unknown Jew living in Persia, who made use of the writings of Mardochai (9:20), the annals of the kings of Persia (2:23; 10:2), and oral traditions dear to his people?

That the book has a true historical kernel is suggested in many ways. There are arguments based on archaeology, topography, chronology, etc. Perhaps the most interesting is the annual observance of the feast of Purim which in the second century before Christ, in the days of the Machabees, was known as Mardochai's day (2 Mac. 15:37). It is still celebrated by the Jews on the 14th Adar (February-March) as a kind of carnival, "a day of feasting, joy and banquets." Friends exchange gifts and alms are given to the poor. The book of Esther is read in the synagogue and all rejoice because God has saved His people.

Bella Chagall has given an unforgettable picture of her childhood memories of this day in Vitebsk. So often has her husband used this little Russian town as background for his intense studies of Christ Crucified that we can easily imagine the small girl running with her brother to the meat market on the square. We watch her as she stands before the white-covered tables on which are spread out before her wondering eyes, a whole world of little Purim objects made of frozen candy — horses, sheep, birds, dolls and golden fiddles. There are bright colored figures of Mardochai and Assuerus that almost seem alive. In *Burning Lights* Marc Chagall has made a pen and ink sketch of the messenger who carried Bella's plate of Purim gifts to her friend who was meant to choose what she wanted and return the plate with a little gift of her own.

In some countries it was the custom to give a Purim play as part of the day's merrymaking. But the most famous of all plays about the deliverance of the Jews from their enemies had another origin. It was written by Racine.

IF YOU REMAIN SILENT

Esther's humble prayer to the Lord God of Israel in which she begs Him to help her people and to take away her fear (14:1–19) was chosen by Racine, the most perfect of French tragic poets, to be the climax of the first act of his play in honor of the Jewish heroine. The daughters of poor nobles, who took parts in the beautiful drama which Racine wrote especially for them, must have been reminded by their teachers of the lessons it contained: the victory of virtue over vice, the power of a good woman, the need to help others, no matter how great the cost, the efficacy of God's care for those who trust Him.

The play was a great success. Louis XIV and his court came to Saint-Cyr from nearby Versailles for the first performance in 1689. So often was it repeated that Madame de Maintenon became alarmed for the little actresses — the oldest was 17 — and so she would not allow outsiders to attend the performance of *Athalie*, based on chapters from the book of Kings, that Racine wrote for them at her request a year later.

Esther has been played many times since the days of the "Sun King." Its truths deserve to be pondered in prayer today. God's work of love calls for apostles willing to collaborate with Christ in the redemption of the world. Comfortable security and selfish isolation are not possible for one who loves his neighbor and knows his neighbor's need. Mardochai understood this when he sent this message to Esther, who was then queen: "Think not that you can save your life in the royal palace. . . . For if you remain silent now the Jews will be saved in some other way, but you and your father's house will perish; and who knows whether you have come to royal estate for such a time as this?" (4:13f.).

ESTHER IN DURA-EUROPAS

Artists as well as playwrights have turned to the book of Esther for inspiration. Most interesting are the murals of the west wall of the synagogue at Dura-Europas. When the Sassanians besieged this city on the right bank of the Euphrates between Damascus and Bagdad in 256 A.D., the Romans covered some of the buildings near the city wall with a mud brick embankment to strengthen the fortifications. Not until the 1930's did an expedition from Yale University take away the protective mud and brick and excavate the prayer hall, the forecourt and adjacent chambers. On the synagogue walls were found some of the earliest known extensive representations of biblical scenes.

In the Esther panel there are three groups. The first is the triumph of Mardochai who is seated on a white horse and led by Aman. The second is, perhaps, the condemnation of Aman. And the third represents Esther's intervention and the countermanding of the decree for the massacre of the Jews (cf. 6:11; 7:9; 8:8–14).

THE GREAT DRAMA OF LOVE

When in 1886 Paul Claudel stood in the cathedral of Notre Dame in Paris on Christmas afternoon he was given an understanding of the childhood, of the eternal innocence, the infinite purity of God. This was the beginning of a journey that was to take him round the world and it was the beginning of a long literary career in which he tried to deepen his initial insight and to share his incommunicable revelation with other men.

At first he sought for help from the world and the men and women around him, then he turned to saintly souls who seemed to have shared experiences similar to his own, and during his last years he seemed to find the answer in all its strength, truth and beauty in the Bible. To speak of the Bible and to bring others to love the Bible was his greatest joy until his death.

That dark, rainy December afternoon in 1886 when he returned home, he opened a Bible. And in his last years it was often in his hands, but his knowledge was never that of a trained scholar. Exegetes reproach him for a disregard for the literal meaning of sacred Scripture and a failure to appreciate scientific research, but there are poetic insights of rare loveliness for those who search his words with care.

He has written a delightful essay on Esther, the great drama of love. This distinguished playwright has cast his study in the form of a play of four acts. His pattern has been adapted here as a suggestion for those who would like to read Esther as did the great Catholic author and diplomat:

Act I
The great banquets and Queen Vasthi's disgrace   1:1–12

Act II
The crowning of Queen Esther   2:1–20

Act III
Scene (1) Mardochai saves the king's life   2:21–23
Scene (2) Mardochai arouses Aman's anger   3:1–6
Scene (3) Aman's revenge   3:7–15

Act IV

Scene (1) Mardochai's appeal to Esther   4:1–17
Scene (2) The reading of the royal annals   6:1–11
Scene (3) The queen's intercession   7:1–10

HE HAS EXALTED THE HUMBLE

Grace, beauty, queenly dignity and power of intercession make Esther
a worthy figure of our Blessed Mother. And the Church does not hesitate to apply to Mary some texts from this book. The seventh responsory
of the feast of Our Lady of Lourdes is an adaptation of Mardochai's
plea to Esther: "Do thou therefore call upon the Lord and speak to the
King for us and deliver us from death" (15:3). The eighth antiphon is
also from this book: "Fear not, for this law was not made for you but
for all others" (15:13). The communion verse in a Mass of Our Lady
Mediatrix reads: "Most wonderful are you, Mary, in your countenance
is every grace" (15:17).

Three other liturgical texts are worth noting. Mardochai's prayer to
his sovereign Lord who is King of all things is read in the lesson of the
third Wednesday in Lent. The gradual gives us the theme of this prayer
in the words of Psalm 27: "Lord, save Your people, and bless Your
chosen flock. To You I cry aloud, do not leave my cry unanswered, or
I am no better than a dead man going down to the grave" (9:1). The
introit for the twenty-first Sunday after Pentecost is a perfect act of
confidence: "All things, O Lord, are in Your power and there is none
that can resist Your will. Heaven and earth and all things under the
vault of heaven are Your creation. You are Lord of all" (13:9ff.). The
offertory of the following Sunday is Esther's prayer as she went to
Xerxes and begged God to frame her plea so that the king would look
with favor upon her words.

Two final references must be noted. They are phrases that recur in
the *Magnificat*. In Mardochai's dream he is shown that the humble are
exalted: "He hath put down the mighty from their thrones and exalted
the humble" (cf. 11:11) and Mardochai in exhorting Esther reminds
her of her lowliness. Like Mary she is one of Yahweh's loved ones, "a
poor little one of Israel" (cf. 15:2).

GOD PAYS EVERY DEBT

When the soul begins to taste the joys of divine union, it cries out with
St. John of the Cross that it is indeed recompensed for all its past trials.
In the words of the "Living Flame of Love," God "pays every debt."

The saint borrows an example from the book of Esther to show what he means:

    And thus the soul that aforetime was without (like Mardochai, weeping in the streets of Susa because his life was in peril, and clothed in sackcloth . . .) is recompensed in a single day for all its trials and services, for not only is it made to enter the palace and stand before the king, clothed in regal vesture, but likewise is it crowned, and given a sceptre, and a royal seat, and possession of the king's ring. It is as another Esther so that it may do all that it desires, and need do naught that it desires not to do in the kingdom of its Spouse. For those that are in this state receive all that they desire. The soul is recompensed for the whole debt, since its enemies are now dead — namely the desires that were going about to take away its life — and it now lives in God.

THIS LAW IS NOT FOR THEE

Such a privileged soul knows that whatever good it possesses comes from God. In honoring the soul, God is honoring His own gifts, or as St. John of the Cross puts it, quoting from the book of Esther: "Worthy of such honor is he whom the King is pleased to honor."

This master of the spiritual life referred to this queen on another occasion, when he considered the consequences of the realization of God's divine beauty: the soul cannot bear the vision of divine beauty any more than could Esther, who fainted when she looked upon the monarch in all his majesty and he seemed to her "like an angel and his face was full of grace."

It is comforting to read the rest of chapter 15 and to meditate on the king's words: "What is the matter, Esther? . . . You should not die, for this law is not made for you. . . . Come near and touch the golden scepter. . . ."

This scene has reminded spiritual writers of Mary's immaculate conception and of her intercessory power. She, on whom the penalty of original sin was not imposed, is sinful man's most powerful intercessor. She can "touch the golden scepter," that is, she can exercise the rights promised her by the King who has given her, as Xerxes gave Esther, half His kingdom. The Fathers like to think that Christ the Judge has reserved justice as His portion and surrendered the other half of His kingdom, that is, the divine mercy, to our Queen, His Mother.

PLEAD FOR US THERE IN GOD'S PRESENCE

In September, 1585, El Greco came to Toledo. Six months later he was at work on a painting that now hangs in the Church of San Tomé, not far from his little home in the Tagus valley. The title of the picture is "The Burial of Count Orgaz."

This young nobleman was rich, well-born, well-loved. He died, and his distinguished friends agreed that his had been a life of unusual holiness. In the crowded church of San Tomé on the day of his funeral appeared a bishop and a deacon whom the aristocratic Spaniards had never seen before. Reverently the celestial strangers performed the last rites for the saintly young man. The Christians of Toledo quickly identified the two strangers: St. Augustine, the bishop of Hippo, and Stephen, the young deacon who, "filled with the Holy Ghost," had seen just before his own death the heavens open and Jesus standing at God's right hand in all the glory of the heavenly court.

This was the scene the canons of San Tomé asked El Greco to paint. The canvas is divided into two parts. In the lower section, St. Augustine and St. Stephen in full pontificals respectfully lay the richly clad Count Orgaz to rest. The Toledan noblemen who surround the corpse evince only the slightest, well-bred surprise at the presence of the two saints. It is but fitting, their refined attitude seems to signify, that such an honor should be paid to one of us.

Above their highly aristocratic and serenely self-satisfied faces we see, what they cannot, the opened heavens where the dead Count is being judged. The upper part of the canvas is crowded with angels and saints, all tremendously and intensely concerned about the poor man's fate. No longer is he the complacent, well-built, luxuriously clothed aristocrat. The purifying experience of death has stripped him of all the externals upon which the world bases its judgments. Now, a beggar in rags, kneeling before his Judge, he raises his long, bony arms and points to our Lady, humbly acknowledging that it is through her all-powerful intercession that he is saved. As Henri Ghéon has written: "With deep humility she deprecates this, but she cannot prevent her whole body (seemingly lost in her swirling cloak), her beautiful hands, her pure and noble face, from portraying the power of mercy which she has won and which she holds over the heart of God."

Her Son, too, points to her as to another Esther and we can hear the words that have been repeated through the centuries: "What will you have, my Queen? What is your request? . . . It shall be given you."

In prayer before this powerful picture we do well to repeat the words of Jeremias (18:20), which the Church places on our lips on many of Mary's feasts: "Virgin, Mother of God, do not forget us, plead for us, there where you stand in God's presence, to turn away from us His wrath."

As we study this dramatic portrayal of Mary interceding for a soul redeemed by her Son, we are reminded of the introit of the feast of her most Immaculate Heart. Without fear we can go through the sunshine and shadow of each day, and come to the portals of death, knowing that one more brave, more beautiful, more holy than Esther will speak for us to the King: "Let us therefore draw near with confidence to the throne of grace so that we may obtain mercy and find grace in time of need."

THE BOOKS OF MACHABEES

MATHATHIAS was dying. To the loyal Jews who had followed the old priest into the mountains south of Jerusalem this seemed the end of their struggle against the Syrians. To his five sons, who stood at his side, this meant the more complete dedication of their lives and strength to the observance of the Law, the re-establishment of the Covenant and the expulsion of the pagan foe.

For this was the command the old man gave them. Their models were to be Abraham whom God had tested and whose trustfulness was never darkened by doubt, Joseph who could keep God's law when alone in a land of disbelief, Phinees so great a lover of purity that he and his descendants had earned the right of an inalienable priesthood forever, Josue whose loyal service was rewarded with the rule of Israel, David mighty warrior and tender friend of God whose dynasty will never fail.

With the example of the heroes of their race the old priest reminded his sons that no man ever wants for strength if his trust be firmly centered in God; so bidding them take their brother Judas as their leader and bring their country redress, he blessed them and died. This was the beginning of the long fight for freedom whose significant story is told in the books of the Machabees.

FRIENDLY PERSUASION

Antiochus IV, the Syrian ruler of much of the Mediterranean world, wanted to unify the people of his kingdom by giving them the pagan and material culture that Alexander the Great had brought from Greece. Wherever Hellenism was introduced, morality suffered and spiritual values lost their position of priority. Cicero's grandfather was one day to come to the conclusion that the more fluently a Roman spoke Greek the more likely he was to be a rascal, but the Syrian king met with little opposition when he began to impose Greek customs, language and religious practices on his subject peoples.

Even in Jerusalem the wealthy and progressive Jews adopted the new ways with alacrity. They sent their sons to the recently erected gymnasium and allowed them to take part in programs of physical fitness repugnant to Jewish ideas of modesty. The rich and the well-born wore Greek clothes, spoke the language of Athens, and prided themselves on aping the elegant and polished manners of the Hellenists.

PASSIVE RESISTANCE

Antiochus wanted more than that. He proclaimed himself *Theos Epiphanes*, "God manifest," and stripping the Temple of its treasures, he set up an altar to the Greek god Zeus. To keep the Sabbath, to be circumcised, to possess a copy of sacred Scripture, was to die.

Reaction was immediate. Despite defections in the cities, there was determined resistance throughout the land; this resistance was first passive, then active.

Passive resistance took the form of a mass exodus to the mountain country south of Jerusalem. The leader was Mathathias, a humble priest of the Hasmonean family whose descendants were to rule Israel for more than a century, that is, until an unworthy Hasmonean woman became the wife of Herod the Great. An intrepid love of the Law inspired these followers of Mathathias, men who were willing to die for the Sinaitic Covenant which God had made with the nation and kept so faithfully with their fathers.

ACTIVE RESISTANCE

Thoughtful men realized that more energetic measures must be taken. They turned to the leader whom Mathathias had given them and found that God had blessed his choice. Natural causes alone cannot account for the victories of the small band of fighters whom Judas pitted so skillfully against the long-triumphant armies of the Syrian king.

While maintaining its religious character, the movement developed into a national revolt that sought to free the country from the rule of Antiochus and his successors. National unity alone would ensure religious freedom, so the struggle was twofold. Judas and his brothers fought against their own people who had succumbed to the Greek ways of the Syrians, and they fought against the Syrians. In both conflicts they were successful.

VICTORY

To Judas was given the title of Machabeus which is probably derived from the Aramaic word *maqqaba* which means "hammer," because of the crushing blows with which he smote the enemy. The success of his brothers won for them the same glorious epithet, which was extended to their descendants and to those who shared their dangers and enjoyed their triumphs.

Jerusalem was captured, the Temple was cleansed, once again morning and evening sacrifices were offered as Moses had prescribed. Jonathan succeeded his brother Judas who was treacherously slain; Simon succeeded his brother Jonathan who was lured, in his turn, to a dastardly death.

The Syrians acknowledged the independence of the new Jewish commonwealth in 142 B.C. and the Romans — to prove their friendship with the newly independent race whose struggle they had been following with interest — sent a letter of confirmation to the rulers and the peoples of the East. Not until eighty years later would the Jews be incorporated in the Roman Empire.

Simon, the brother of Judas, enjoyed all the privileges and trappings of royalty, but he did not claim the title of king. "The Jews and their priests consented that he be their prince and high priest forever, until there should arise a faithful prophet" (1 Mac. 14:41). He was not called king because without a special sign from God no one dared replace the family of David by a new dynasty. The "weeks" counted out by Daniel were coming to an end. Belief in the coming Messias was strong in many hearts.

Simon's reign was a fitting prelude to the kingdom of the Great King. "He made peace in the land, and Israel rejoiced with great joy. Every man sat under his vine and under his fig tree. There was none to make them afraid. There was none left in the land to fight against them" (1 Mac. 14:8ff.). The sons of Mathathias had proved worthy of their father's trust.

THE FIRST BOOK OF MACHABEES

This is the story read in the breviary during October. The first book of Machabees gives the history of the whole struggle from the reign of Antiochus IV (175 B.C.) until the death, in 135, of Simon Machabee, prince and high priest of his people. The second book, by another author with another purpose and another point of view, describes incidents that took place during the first years of revolt (175–161).

What do we know about the author of the first book? Very little. He was a devout and patriotic man. He knew and loved his country. He wrote of battles with the skill of a competent and experienced fighter. The literary value of the original Hebrew or Aramaic document must have been high but only Greek translations are extant. Although he cites official documents, his work is not a compilation but the pleasant and easily read reminiscences of a Jew who observed the Law faithfully, who rejoiced in its victories, and who reported what he had seen with the unexpected objectivity of the true historian.

THE SECOND BOOK OF MACHABEES

The author of the second book was more of a preacher than a historian. His aim was to edify rather than to inform. As a vehicle for his pious exhortations he chose to make a digest of a five volume Greek history of the Machabean revolt composed by a certain Jason of Cyrene. His aim was to acquaint the Jews of Egypt with religious issues rather than to tell them about matters military or political.

To him the climax of the uprising was the institution of two feasts. The first was the feast of the Dedication of the Temple which was kept every year in December to commemorate "with joy and gladness" the purification of the temple after its idolatrous profanation by the Syrians.

It was on the occasion of this feast, about two centuries later, that the Jews put the most momentous of all questions to our Lord in these words: "If Thou art the Christ tell us openly." And in answer He stated His divine Sonship so clearly that no soul in good faith from that day to this can be in any doubt: "I and the Father are one." It was for this that the Jews sought to stone Him but He escaped from the temple. His hour had not yet come (John 10:22–39).

The second feast is that of Nicanor's Holiday — an annual celebration in honor of the recapture of the holy city. The watchwords of the Machabees for this triumph had been "Help is from God," and "With God the victory." Their method, too, deserves to be noted, for it is well worth making our own. We are told that "while fighting with their hands, they prayed with their hearts" and in their combat they were "greatly cheered with the presence of God."

These two books have never been accepted by the Jews as part of their Bible. About their divine origin there was, at first, some doubt. But the Fathers recognized them as inspired and the Church, confident of the help their dramatic lesson will bring us, has placed them in our hands.

DOCTRINAL LESSONS

It is when we examine the theology of the two books that startling differences are at once apparent.

The name of *Yahweh* found more than 6700 times in the Old Testament is not mentioned once in the first book despite the author's love of the Law and the temple. It is replaced by nouns or adjectives such as Heaven, the Name, or the Eternal.

The author of the second book has centered his work about God and the names he employs make a lovely litany. God is All Powerful, the Most High, the Liberator, the Savior, the All-Knowing One, the Living One, the Merciful One, the Just Judge, the Creator of the World, the Worker of Miracles, the Lord of Heaven, the King of Kings, the Father. The author refers to Israel as the people of God, the chosen people, God's inheritance, the holy people. Suffering to him is medicinal, because God pities and never abandons His own.

The true dogmatic importance of the book is to be found in its unequivocal teaching about the resurrection of the dead, the efficacy of prayer, the intercession of the saints, rewards and punishments after death.

THE PATRIMONY OF THE MACHABEES

Both authors show that the true patrimony of the Machabees is to be found in the Sinaitic Covenant, the Mosaic Law, the psalms, the words of the prophets, the observance of the Sabbath and all days of fast and prayer, as well as their dear and long established rites and customs. The picture which they give of the rugged courage of God's people is a help to every reader — for we, too, are in the militant service of the same Master.

They are good models for us in many ways. Their love of the Bible should be ours: Jonathan was able to reject help proffered by the Spartans with these words: "For ourselves, we have little need of such things, having for our comfort the holy books that are in our hands" (1 Mac. 12:9). In moments of danger we would do well to study the thought with which Judas rallied some of the less valiant who proposed prudent flight: "God forbid that we do this thing, and flee . . . ; but if our time be come let us die manfully for our brethren, and let us not stain our glory" (1 Mac. 9:10).

There is even a lesson to be found in the account of the suicide of Razias (2 Mac. 14:37–46). This passage, so puzzling to the moralists, tells how a Jerusalem elder was resolved to die rather than risk apostasy. They condemn his deed and praise his motive. We, without condoning what he did, will do well to remember that it is a greater treason "to do the right deed for the wrong reason."

When the beauty-loving Renaissance Pope, Julius II, asked Raphael to decorate one of the high ceilinged rooms of the Vatican, he assigned to that lovable artist the theme: "God protects His Church."

Those who have visited what is now known as "the Room of Heliodorus" have discovered that Raphael turned to the Old Testament and chose to paint an incident from the book of Machabees: the expulsion of Heliodorus, the minister sent by the king of Syria to seize the temple treasure.

With richness of tone, depth of color, and vigorous modeling, Raphael portrays a scene of swift and brilliant movement. The courts of the temple are crowded with terrified men, women and children who, with prayer and penance, implore miraculous deliverance. The foreign envoys are plundering the Holy of Holies. Onias, the high priest, kneels in prayer. Warrior angels rush though the air. A golden-armored rider of a royally caparisoned horse had cast the rapacious Syrian to the ground and painfully wounded him. Thus was God's protective power manifest (2 Mac. 3:27).

Let us examine in somewhat greater detail the heroic stature of Judas, the first Machabean leader. Then we will consider the two examples that Origen chose to steady the courage of persecuted Christians in his *Exhortation to Martyrdom*: the death of Eleazar and the story of the seven holy Machabees. But this is not to exhaust the riches of these books as the list of recommended readings will show.

SUGGESTED READING

JUDAS MACHABEUS

Men of every nation find much to admire in the Machabean leader. Handel composed a majestic oratorio with brilliant musical contrasts to show the desperate situation out of which his courage had fashioned final victory. Longfellow wrote a drama that gives us a leader who could understand his enemies and infuse in his followers something of his own intrepid spirit. Calderon stresses his honor, his loyalty and the wholehearted intensity with which he fought.

Dante found him among the heroes of Mars, in the heaven of martyrs, where these great men, with true nobility of soul, attributed to God all credit for their earthly triumphs, singing: "Not to us, Lord, but to Thy Name be the praise for the glory wrought in us." Botticelli in his illustration of this scene has given in flowing line and rhythmic movement the calm detachment and inner fire so characteristic of Judas. They convey, too, Dante's message that happiness is not to be found alone in the contemplation of the truths of theology but we must add act to thought, and follow the examples set for us by Judas and all valiant men.

In him were united the qualities of true leadership: a serene and penetrating intellect, a will of firm determination, never failing thought for others, plus the motive of a great cause. He blamed no one and asked for nothing from his men that he was not willing to give. He could well say:

All make all:
For while I leave one muscle of my strength
Undisturbed, or hug one coin of ease
Or private peace while the huge debt of pain
Mounts over all the earth,
Or, fearing for myself, take half a stride
Where I could leap: while any hour remains
Indifferent, I have no right or reason
To raise a cry against this blundering cruelty
Of man.[1]

[1] Quoted with permission of the Oxford University Press from Christopher Fry's *Thor, with Angels.*

His care for his men did not stop with his example and his thoughtful provisions for their day-to-day needs. He was mindful of them after
death, as we see in the epistle read in the second Mass on the feast of
All Souls and repeated in every anniversary Mass. There it is related
how Judas, after defeating Gorgias, collected twelve thousand pieces
of silver and sent them to Jerusalem "to have sacrifice made in atonement for the dead men's sins" (2 Mac. 12:43–46). St. Thomas makes
"this holy and wholesome" remembrance of the departed Machabees
the basis for his affirmative answer to the question: "Whether the dead
can be assisted by the works of the living" (*Sup.* 71, 2).

Men now honor Judas, but this was not always true during his lifetime. His last days were marked by failure that God sometimes uses to
test those He loves. His men deserted him. His friends counseled him
to avoid battle. His messengers told him of treason throughout the land.
He refused to seek safety in flight and he fell in battle. Too late, the
people mourned their great warrior. "How is the mighty one fallen,"
they cried, "the great savior of Israel."

TO DIE AGAIN

To keep the Law of Moses meant a martyr's death. As always in times
of general danger cowardly men wavered and fell; men with vision met
death with ready resolve, bequeathing to their people the power of their
own high courage.

Eleazar was one of the Jews who faced this trial unflinchingly. He
was a leader of the scribes, a man of great age and great influence. As
a sign of conformity with the new regime he was required to eat pork,
food forbidden by Moses. Old friends with misplaced pity, taking him
aside, desired that he send for meat that he could taste without a
scruple, assuring him that the king would be satisfied with this pre-
tended obedience. Arguments, threats and promises failed to move him.
He withstood them all.

Faithful to the Law which he had observed conscientiously from
childhood, the old man of ninety years would have none of these cowardly subterfuges, saying that younger men might weaken were he to
give bad example. He preferred death with honor to life with shame.
Man's punishments, he said, can be evaded, but no one can escape the
almighty hand of God.

Enraged at his words the king's men led him to the place of execu-
tion, and, as he lay dying under the lash, his last words were: "O Lord,

in Thy wisdom, Thou knowest that I might have had life if I would, yet
never a cruel pang my body endures, but my soul suffers it gladly out
of reverence for Thee" (cf. 2 Mac. 6:30f.).

GOD'S SCHOOLING

So brave and honorable a death was to breed courage in other hearts.
Seven brothers were at that time under arrest. Their mother was with
them. They, too, were told to eat unclean food. The eldest said to the
king: "We would rather die than break the Law God gave our fathers."
Provoked at this fearless answer, the king commanded that the speaker
be wounded in hands and feet and tongue, and be cast into a brazen
vessel set amidst a blazing fire. Heartened by the prayers of his six
brothers and his mother, the young man died a martyr.

The guards turned to the second brother. Tortures, exceeding those
inflicted on the first, drew from his dying lips this act of faith: "Men
may take mortal life from us; but the King of the world will raise us up,
who die for His laws, in the resurrection of eternal life."

The third, when it was his turn, confidently put forth his tongue and
offered his hands to his assailants, saying: "These I have from heaven,
but for the Law of God, I despise them: because I hope to receive them
again from Him." When it was time for the fourth to die, he declared:
"It is better, being put to death by men, to look for hope from God."
So they came to the fifth. Gallantly he bore his pain, warning the king
that God's wrath would one day be visited upon the monarch and those
dear to him, while God's blessings would reward those who place all
hope in Him. The sixth son, as intrepid as his brothers, acknowledged
humbly that for their sins they deserved torments and a lingering death,
but it were vain for the king to think that he could defy God and remain
unpunished therefor.

The king made no answer but he considered the seventh son. Perhaps, he thought, blandishments and bribes will break this young man's
mettle. Wealth, power and pleasure, he promised in exchange for apostasy. The boy was unimpressed. The king summoned the mother and
counselled her to advise her child. She did so, bending over him and
entreating him with these words: "I beseech thee, my son, look upon
heaven and earth, and all that is in them. Consider that God made them
out of nothing, mankind, also. So shalt thou not fear this tormentor,
but being made a worthy partner with thy brothers, receive death, so
shall the divine mercy give me back all my sons at once." The young

martyr did not listen to the end but cried out to his executioners: "For whom do you wait? I do not obey the command of the king but the command of the divine Law given us by Moses."

To the king he said: "If we grievously suffer, grievously have we sinned. The Lord our God schools and corrects us. After brief pain my brothers now enjoy eternal life. Soon the anger of the Almighty which has justly fallen on our nation shall cease."

So he died trusting wholly in the Lord. His mother, who with wisdom and resolution had strengthened each of her sons, joining "a man's heart to a woman's thought," went to her own death unafraid (2 Mac. 7).

Their feast is observed liturgically in the universal Church. Each year at their Mass we beg them to obtain for us "an increase of faith," "fresh power," "deeper joy" and the grace to follow steadfastly their strength-giving example. By the Russian peasant, these martyrs were once, and perhaps still are, honored as powerful intercessors and it was an often repeated saying: "Rain on Machabees (August first) means no fires this year."

Although it is clearly stated in the Martyrology that the holy remains of the Machabees were taken to Rome, the location of these relics was not known until the last century. In 1876 repairs made to the pavement before the high altar of St. Peter in Chains disclosed a centuries old sarcophagus divided neatly into compartments and marked with two carefully worded plaques attesting that the long lost relics of the Machabees were within.

It is a sobering experience to kneel before this primitive coffin; to examine the Gospel scenes carved so starkly on its surface and to realize that the martyrs whose ashes have apparently been so long preserved here knew none of the lessons of our Lord's teaching that are cut on the smooth stone. Our helps being the greater, can our service be less generous than theirs?

THE COVENANT GOD MADE WITH OUR FATHERS

It would be to misread the books of Machabees to see in their pages merely the adventures of men fired with love of God and country. Their real meaning is hidden in the words which the priest pronounces over the wine at the moment of consecration: "This is the chalice of My blood of the new and eternal covenant." The covenant which Christ made with all mankind on the cross and renews in the holy Sacrifice of the Mass is "new and eternal." It replaces the old covenant made by

God with Noe, with the patriarchs, and particularly with the Hebrew
nation through Moses on Mount Sinai. In exchange for His protection
His chosen people had promised to keep His Law, to worship Him and
love Him.

There had been many vicissitudes. Out of Egypt God had led them.
In the desert He had formed them. Judges, kings and prophets had
pointed the way of loyal service. Chastened by the Babylonian exile,
disciplined by foreign rulers, they had discovered by centuries of experience that God's mercy is limitless and His chastisements have no
other meaning than love.

Now the years of the Law and the temple were drawing to an end.
Those who had learned the lesson were given one last chance to make
ready for the New Law and "the Temple not made with hands." The
preparations begun in Genesis are completed in Machabees. The message of the last book of the Old Testament repeats the teaching of the
first: God made us to love and serve Him.

LOVE THAT DARES AND ENDURES

To one who loves God, this story of the successful resistance of the
Machabees is a challenge and an inspiration. It is the story of a love
strong enough to undertake and endure great things. In the *Summa* we
learn that the name for love like this is *fortitude*. To dread no hardship,
not even death, for the sake of the one loved is to possess fortitude and
with it the four beautiful virtues of which it is composed. If these are
ours no sorry failure will mar our lives, whatever be the issue.

Magnanimity is the first of these virtues — the stretching forth of the
mind to great things, assured and hopeful of success. *Magnificence* is
another—the accomplishment of noble deeds with high, untroubled
resolution. When victory seems doubtful the soul needs *patience*, the
willed endurance of the painfully difficult, and *perseverance* which is
firm persistence in a well considered purpose.

All these God gave the men who tried to keep His Law, to overcome
His foes, to establish His kingdom. All these He will give us, if we ask,
because the task which His Son, dying on the cross, entrusted to us,
is the same.

INDEX

158